FOR THE SWIFTIES:

A PUZZLE BOOK INSPIRED BY **TAYLOR SWIFT**

(UNOFFICIAL VERSION)

SPHERE
First published in Great Britain in 2024 by Sphere
1 3 5 7 9 10 8 6 4 2

A CIP catalogue record for this book
is available from the British Library.

ISBN 978-1-4087-3416-2

Designed by D.R. ink
Printed and bound in Great Britain by Clays Ltd, Elcograf S.p.A.

Papers used by Sphere are from well-managed forests
and other responsible sources.

Sphere
An imprint of
Little, Brown Book Group
Carmelite House
50 Victoria Embankment
London EC4Y 0DZ

An Hachette UK Company
www.hachette.co.uk

www.littlebrown.co.uk

FOR THE SWIFTIES:
A PUZZLE BOOK INSPIRED BY TAYLOR SWIFT

(UNOFFICIAL VERSION)

AIDA ALONZO

SPHERE

FOR THE
SWIFTIES

A NOTE ON THE PUZZLES

American spelling has been used throughout this book in keeping with the spelling Taylor uses in her lyrics, e.g. labour is labor, favourite is favorite. Bear this in mind as you journey through the book.

For each puzzle, you'll find a key.

The puzzle piece denotes how hard the puzzle is:
1 (easy), 2 (medium) or 3 (hard).

The cat denotes the level of Swiftiness needed to complete the puzzle: 1 (basic), 2 (mid-level) or 3 (Swift-tastic).

NOTE FROM THE AUTHOR

Taylor Swift has felt like a treasured friend for years, from when I was a teenager in my bedroom belting out *Stay Beautiful* on my thrift shop guitar, to today, listening to *the tortured poets department* on repeat while I construct puzzles. It's always an honor when a friend trusts me with their inner world. Taylor Swift lifts me out of mine and into hers, moving me to alternately dance, weep and wonder as we voyage through her castles, forests, heartaches and hopes. I love spending time in the secret gardens of her mind, where she sings about emotions and experiences that mirror my own, giving them a clearer shape and value. And her openness feels extra generous because it's not just in a private relationship with me: it's for all of us. Over the years it has catalyzed new connections and deepened friendships with fellow Swifties. This project has been a joyful example of that. When I started putting this book together, I sounded the bugle horn to all the Swifties I know, and they enthusiastically rallied round to pitch in their creative ideas.
I hope this book is an enjoyable outlet for Swifties to celebrate this extraordinary woman's art and a way for others to get to know the phenomenon and mastermind that is Taylor Swift. Come play with us in the gardens – it's beautiful here!

INTRODUCTION

deAr Reader,

welcome! this is thE ultimate puzzle book for taYlor swift fans everywhere. it's filled with crOsswords, sUdoklus, cRyptograms, wordsEarches, quizzes, mAzes, magic, maDness, heaven and sin. come with **eYes open**; some of these puzzles are **treacherous**ly hard. but rest assured, there is something For everyone in here, and unlike in the real world, the answers are in the back, sO you can always **begin again** if you get stuck down a dead end. i know **all too well** that after yeaRs of hunting easter eggs and decoding the clues that taylor has left for us, you are ready for combat when It comes to cracking codes and unTangling puzzles! **don't you**? So let the games begin!

wishing you the **best day**,

love,

aida

SINGONYMS

WHICH TAYLOR SWIFT SONG TITLES ARE HIDDEN IN THESE SYNONYMS?

1. Untamed Fantasies

2. Strikes In A New Way

3. Escape Vehicle

4. Residential Heroes

5. The Littlest Guy That Existed at Any Point

6. Remain Gorgeous

7. A Flawlessly Excellent Cardiac Organ

8. Two Weeks

9. Romance Narrative

10. Milky Steed

11. Explain To Me The Reason

12. Leap And After, Collapse

13. Enter Inside With The Precipitation

SPELLING VAULT

SPELLING IS FUN!

Join Taylor in her love of words and find as many as you can using the central letter. Each word must have a minimum of four letters and letters can be used more than once. For bonus points, find the Taylor related word from the vault which uses all the letters!

4-letter words:

5-letter words:

6-letter words:

7-letter words:

8-letter word:

'TIS THE DAMN SEASON

TAYLOR'S SONGS CAN CARRY US THROUGH ANY SEASON

Which seasons does she mention in each of the below songs? The total number of songs referencing each season is at the top of each list to help you out. Each song names one season.

Tim McGraw	*Lover*
All Too Well	*marjorie*
august	*Paper Rings*
Better Than Revenge	*peace*
betty	*Red*
Christmas Tree Farm	*seven*
Cornelia Street	*Starlight*
evermore	*Suburban Legends*
Hits Different	*The Best Day*
I Bet You Think About Me	*The Smallest Man Who Ever Lived*
ivy	*You're On Your Own Kid*
Love Story	

FUN FACT: Taylor's *Tim McGraw* music video was shot at Johnny Cash's cabin. She started writing the song during her freshman math class.

Summer (Total = 13)

Fall/Autumn (Total = 5)

Winter (Total = 3)

Spring (Total = 2)

POP QUIZ

1. What year was Taylor born?
    a. 1984   b. 1989   c. 1992

2. What is Taylor's lucky number? This is also the day of the month she was born and the length of the intro of the first song on her first album.
    a. 7   b. 8   c. 13

3. What is Taylor's star sign? In the music video for *Lavender Haze*, there is a shot of a vinyl cover for another of her songs, *Mastermind*, which shows her constellation alongside the constellation for Pisces. This is the star sign of her ex-boyfriend, Joe Alwyn, who she confirmed on Instagram that this song was about.
    a. Sagittarius   b. Scorpio   c. Gemini

4. What is Taylor's middle name?
    a. Elizabeth   b. Emily   c. Alison

5. What is Taylor's mother's name?
    a. Andrea   b. Diana   c. Joan

6. What is Taylor's brother's name?
    a. Alex   b. Brad   c. Austin

7. What's Taylor's brother's nickname for her?
    a. Tay-yay   b. Taffy   c. Blondie

8. What is Taylor's father's name?
    a. Colin   b. Scott   c. Mark

9. What is Taylor's maternal grandmother's name?
    a. Elodie   b. Marjorie   c. Melody

10. What did Taylor's maternal grandmother do for a living?
    a. Opera singing   b. Lace making   c. Cat breeding

11. What is reported to be Taylor's favorite alcoholic drink?
    a. Gin and tonic   b. Vodka diet coke   c. Pornstar martini

12. What has Taylor said she'd order at a drive through?
    a. Cheeseburger, fries, and a chocolate shake
    b. Chicken nuggets and a strawberry shake
    c. Apple pie

13. Which species of arthropod is named after Taylor?
    a. Spider   b. Crab   c. Millipede

14. What has Taylor said is her favorite TV show?

    a. *Game of Thrones* b. *Grey's Anatomy* c. *Friends*

15. What did Taylor tell people she wanted to be when she grew up when she was five?

    a. A stockbroker b. A Christmas tree farmer c. A horse rider

16. What song did Taylor write for a high school talent show during ninth grade?

    a. *Lucky You* b. *Our Song* c. *Tim McGraw*

17. What is the name of Taylor's debut album, released in 2006?

    a. *Enchanted* b. *Taylor Swift* c. *Our Songs*

18. How many copies did Taylor's debut album sell in the first week?

    a. 39,000 b. 56,000 c. 27,000

19. How many copies did *Fearless* sell in the first week?

    a. 700,080 b. 592,000 c. 420,500

20. Which celebrity crush of Taylor's did Ellen DeGeneres surprise Taylor with on *The Ellen DeGeneres Show* in 2008?

    a. Taylor Lautner b. Zac Efron c. Justin Timberlake

21. In which year did Taylor win her first MTV Video Music Award? It was at this event that Kanye famously stormed the stage and took the microphone from Taylor.

    a. 2008 b. 2009 c. 2011

22. In what year did Taylor win her first Grammy award?

    a. 2010 b. 2011 c. 2014

23. In 2010, Taylor famously met with fans for a meet and greet at Bridgestone Arena in Nashville, Tennessee. How many hours was it scheduled for and how long did it wind up taking?

    a. It was scheduled for 1 hour and took 6

    b. It was scheduled for 3 hours and took 8

    c. It was scheduled for 13 hours and took 15

24. In an April 2010 YouTube video titled 'Demonstrating my fine athletic skills. And more.', what type of hunt do Taylor and her friends go on? In it, Taylor states that she's not a very good _____ hunter.

    a. An Easter egg hunt b. A treasure hunt c. A fox hunt

25. In the same video, whose wedding does Taylor go to? This person collaborated with her on hit songs such as *White Horse* and *You Belong With Me*.

    a. LeAnn Rimes b. Liz Rose c. Dolly Parton

26. What was the name of the perfume that Taylor released in 2011?

    a. Wonderstruck b. Enchanted c. Mesmerized

27. Which legendary Swedish songwriter and music producer did Taylor first work with on her album *Red*? He went on to collaborate with Taylor on numerous hits, including *Blank Space* and *Shake It Off*. Other credits include Britney Spears' *...Baby One More Time*, the Backstreet Boys' *I Want It That Way*, Celine Dion's *That's The Way It Is*, and Katy Perry's *I Kissed a Girl*.

    a. Shellback   b. Mark Ronson   c. Max Martin

28. Which of Taylor's songs was the first song to reach number one on the Billboard Hot 100?

    a. *Love Story*

    b. *We Are Never Ever Getting Back Together*

    c. *Shake It Off*

29. How long is the longest song on *Red (Taylor's Version)*? This song became the longest song to hit number 1 on the US Hot 100, unseating Don McLean's American Pie.

    a. 7 minutes   b. 10 minutes   c. 13 minutes

30. Which actor starred in Taylor's *All Too Well: The Short Film*?

    a. Sadie Sink   b. Cara Delevingne   c. Lena Dunham

31. In a 2014 interview with CBS, what three words did Taylor use to describe herself?

    a. Kind, conscientious, insecure

    b. Creative, ambitious, empathetic

    c. Imaginative, smart, hard working

32. Which song on *1989* includes the sound of Taylor's heartbeat?

    a. *Welcome To New York*   b. *Wildest Dreams*   c. *This Love*

33. Which song on *1989* did Taylor reveal was inspired by Jack Antonoff and Lena Dunham's relationship at the time?

    a. *I Wish You Would*   b. *How You Get The Girl*   c. *You Are in Love*

34. Which song on *1989* has Taylor described as a 'sister' of *Out of the Woods* and *Is it Over Now?*

    a. *I Wish You Would*   b. *I Know Places*   c. *Style*

35. What logistical reason meant Taylor could not attend the VMAs in 2016?

    a. It was her mother's 60th birthday party on the same night.

    b. Her jet got stuck in London due to stormy weather.

    c. She had been called for jury duty in Nashville the next morning.

36. Which of Taylor's exes also has a track called *Sweet Nothing*, which was released in October 2012?

    a. John Mayer   b. Calvin Harris   c. Harry Styles

37. Which Swedish pseudonym did Taylor first use in 2016 in the writing credits for *This Is What You Came For*, which she wrote with Calvin Harris?

    a. Nils Sjöberg   b. Hans Andersson   c. Bo Bergman

38. What did Taylor tell Vogue in 2016 she thinks is the most important life lesson for someone to learn?

    a. That trying and failing repeatedly is normal and key to success.

    b. That people who make fun of you for being enthusiastic are probably not having as much fun as you.

    c. That karma is real.

39. *reputation* was the fastest album in history to reach the number one spot on US iTunes. How quickly after its release did this happen?

    a. 1 second   b. 6 minutes   c. 18 minutes

40. Which song was the last music video Taylor released under Big Machine Records?

    a. *Delicate*   b. *Wildest Dreams*   c. *The Man*

41. During the *reputation* Stadium Tour, who did Taylor dedicate each performance of *Dress* to?

    a. Loie Fuller, a revolutionary dancer and actress who created the 'Serpentine Dance' in the late 1800s and fought for artists to own their own work.

    b. William Bowery

    c. Jessica Jones, who made custom dresses for the tour.

42. When *Lover* was number one for six weeks, making it Taylor's fourth album to hold this rank for this period, which other artists' record did she beat?

    a. ABBA   b. The Beatles   c. Coldplay

43. Which song on *Lover* features the Regent Park School of Music's youth choir?

    a. *I Think He Knows*   b. *ME!*   c. *It's Nice To Have A Friend*

44. Which actor's voice can be heard at the very beginning of *London Boy*?

    a. Idris Elba   b. Daniel Craig   c. Gerard Butler

45. Who can be heard counting in the chorus in *Paper Rings*?

    a. Ed Sheeran   b. Scott Swift   c. Jack Antonoff

46. What is the name of Taylor's male alter ego in the music video for *The Man*?

    a. Toxico Masculico   b. Tyler Swift   c. Jordan Belfort

47. What is the name of the 2020 documentary about Taylor?

    a. *Miss Americana*

    b. *Taylor Swift: A Journey Through The Eras*

    c. *mirrorball*

48. What song did Taylor sing to help raise funds for the COVID-19 Solidarity Response Fund as part of the star-studded *One World: Together at Home* special during the pandemic?

    a. *Epiphany*   b. *Soon You'll Get Better*   c. *The Best Day*

49. Taylor has said that *Death By A Thousand Cuts* is inspired by the Netflix film, *Someone Great*, rather than by her own relationship history. Funnily enough, while working on the treatment for the movie, the writer was inspired by a song from Taylor's *1989* album. Which song was this?
     a. *Out Of The Woods*   b. *Bad Blood*   c. *Clean*

50. What has she said her chosen superpower would be?
     a. Flying   b. Speaking to animals   c. Healing people

51. Who are the three characters involved in *folklore's* 'teenage love triangle'?
     a. Augustine, James, and Betty
     b. Chloe, Sam, and Marcus
     c. Alana, Este, and Danielle

52. Who used the pseudonym William Bowery as a co-writer on *folklore*, *evermore*, and *Midnights*?
     a. Ed Sheeran   b. Joe Alwyn   c. Matty Healy

53. Which track on *Midnights* did Taylor say was inspired while watching *Mad Men* and named after a common phrase used in the 50s to describe being in love?
     a. *Labyrinth*   b. *Snow On The Beach*   c. *Lavender Haze*

54. Which song on *Midnights* contains a sample of Taylor's 2016 single *Out of the Woods* from the *1989* album?
     a. *Maroon*   b. *Question...?*   c. *Karma*

55. What song did Taylor tease a line of in her NYU commencement speech, which references breathing in, through, deep and out?
     a. *Midnight Rain*   b. *Sweet Nothing*   c. *Labyrinth*

56. In what 2022 movie did Taylor star alongside Christian Bale and Margot Robbie, playing the role of Elizabeth Meekins, who gets pushed in front of a car by a hitman while trying to investigate her father's death?
     a. *Amsterdam*   b. *Babylon*   c. *Death on the Nile*

57. In November 2023, which Ivy League US College confirmed they would be offering a course, led by a self-confessed Swiftie professor, called 'Taylor Swift and Her World'?
     a. Dartmouth   b. Cornell   c. Harvard

58. Who designed the *Fearless* minidresses that Taylor wears on the Eras Tour, which have a long fringe decorated with hand applied degradé Swarovski crystals?
     a. Versace   b. Roberto Cavalli   c. Chanel

59. Taylor announced the upcoming release of *the tortured poets department* upon receiving a grammy. What number grammy was this for her?
     a. 10   b. 13   c. 22

60. *the tortured poets department* smashed Spotify streaming records, becoming the most streamed album in one week. It also broke the record for the number of streams in a single day upon its release on 19th April 2024. How many streams did it have on that first day?
     a. 30 million   b. 300 million   c. 3 billion

SNAKES AND STONES

CONNECT THE SNAKE'S HEAD AND TAIL TO COMPLETE ITS BODY

The numbers around the outside of the grid tell you how many pieces of snake are to be placed in each row and column. Within each square, the snake can either move in a straight line or turn at a 90-degree angle.

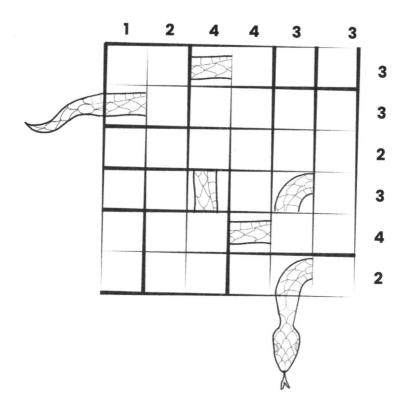

LET'S DRIVE

Write the answer to each question in the corresponding row or column on the crossword below.

ACROSS

4. In which song does Taylor ask the subject of her song to remember when he hit the brakes too fast and ended up having to get stitches in the hospital?

6. In which song does Taylor sing that she was riding in the passenger seat with her hair down in the front of the subject of her song's car?

7. In which song does Taylor sing about boys with expensive cars, such as Range Rovers and Jaguars, and how they never took her quite where her muse did?

8. In which song does Taylor say that she and the subject of her song took a wrong turn and fell into a rabbit hole?

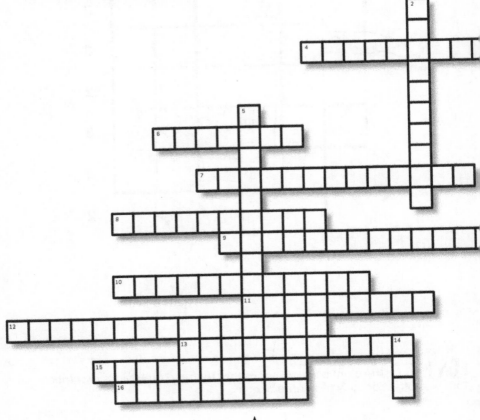

9. In which song does Taylor sing that she hates the pickup truck that the subject of her song never let her drive?

10. In which song does Taylor sing that it's sweet that her muse gets her car door and he pulls her to the back seat?

11. In which song does Taylor sing that her muse is a boy in a Chevy, which often gets stuck on back roads at night?

12. In which song does Taylor imply that the song *Bad Blood* was playing in the cab on her muse's first trip to L.A.?

13. In which song does Taylor sing that she is drunk and crying in the back seat of the car on her way home from the bar?

15. In which song does Taylor say that the subject of her song almost went through a red light because he was looking at her?

16. In which song does Taylor say that what started with a kiss always results in a car tearing out of the drive?

DOWN

1. In which song does Taylor sing that she doesn't know who she'll talk to now at school, but that she knows she'll be laughing in the car on the way home with the subject of her song?

2. In which song does Taylor sing that that she was sitting in a getaway car with the subject of her song and that she could hear sirens in his heartbeat?

3. In which song does Taylor sing that she remembers the subject of her song driving to her house in the middle of the night, and that she's the one who makes him laugh when he knows he's going to cry?

5. The name of this song is the place Taylor casually says she rents, while in the car.

14. In which song does Taylor describe loving her muse as driving a new Maserati along a street with only one way in or out?

FUN FACT CRYPTOGRAM

USE THE CODE BELOW TO REVEAL AN ENCRYPTED FUN FACT ABOUT TAYLOR

Some of the letters have been filled in for you. Work out the code by considering the placement of the letters you already know, revealing a hidden message. Use the key below to track which letters are linked to each number.

A	B	C	D	E	F	G	H	I	J	K	L	M
4								13		10		
N	O	P	Q	R	S	T	U	V	W	X	Y	Z
	8				23			7			25	

```
 _   A   Y   _   O   _        _   A   S       A          _   _   A   _   _   _        _   _   O   _   O
26   4  25  18   8  24       15   4  23       4          9  24   4   5  21   2       14  15   8  26   8

 O   _          _   _   _        _   O   _   _   _   _        K   A   _   Y   _        _   _   S   _
 8   9         26  15  21        5   8   5  21   3  26       10   4   3  25  21       11  21  23  26

 _   I   _   A   _   K   _   _        _   _   _        A   _   _   _   _   _        A   _   _   _
15  13   6   4   1  10  21   2       15  21  24        4   1   1  21  14  26        4   3   1  21

 S   _   _   _   _   _        _   _   _   I   _   _        _   _   _        2   0   0   9
23  14  21  21   1  15        2  22  24  13   3  20       26  15  21

 V   _   A   S       I   _        _   _   _        _   I   V   I   _   _        _   O   O   _        I   _
 7   5   4  23      13   3       15  21  24       18  13   7  13   3  20       24   8   8   5       13   3

 _   A   S   _   V   I   _   _   _   _        _   A   _   _   I   _   _        A   _   O   V   _        A
 3   4  23  15   7  13  18  18  21       15   4   3  20  13   3  20        4  12   8   7  21        4

 _   A   _   _   _   _   I   _   _   _   _        _   O   _   _        _   _   A   _
15   4   3   2  11  24  13  26  26  21   3        3   8  26  21       26  15   4  26

 _   _   A   _   S   :        _   I   _   _        I   S        _   _   _   _        O   _
24  21   4   2  23           18  13   9  21       13  23        9  22  18  18        8   9

 _   I   _   _   _   _        I   _   _   _   _   _   _   _   _        I   O   _   S   .
18  13  26  26  18  21       13   3  26  21  24  24  22  14  26  13   8   3  23
```

ONCE UPON A TIME

MATCH THE TIMES TO THE SONG THEY'RE MENTIONED IN

Better Man

Electric Touch

I Bet You Think About Me

I Wish You Would

Mine

Last Kiss

Lavender Haze

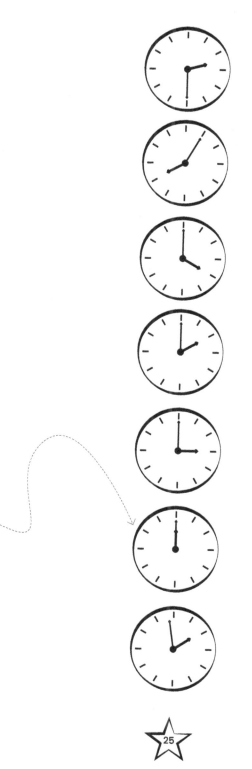

BIG, OLD CITIES

TAYLOR SURE DID REACH HER GOAL OF LIVING IN A BIG OLD CITY SOMEDAY!

Find some of Taylor's stomping grounds from songs in the wordsearch on the opposite page.

Los Angeles

Beverly Hills

Hollywood

Sunrise Boulevard

Sunset and Vine

New York

Centennial Park

Central Park Lake

Chelsea Hotel

Coney Island

Cornelia Street

East Side

High Line

Madison Square

Manhattan

Upstate

West Side

West Village

London

Bond Street

Brixton

Camden Market

Hackney

Highgate

Shoreditch

Soho

The Black Dog

The Heath

The West End

```
X U T B U P S T A T E H R C S J F X F B
K H M H E U J E X Y V A T O C Y I Q J R
I Q F A E A N W T A E C H N H B I J E I
B W O M D B S U R M S K E E E Z N K M X
O E E S Y I L T R Z O N H Y L B V J J T
N X C S U C S A S D H E E I S T P C P O
D V C E T N E O C I O Y A S E H W A L N
S U O R N V R N N K D W T L A E E M O P
T B R H A T I I T S D E H A H W S D S Y
R E N O L S R L S E Q O N N O E T E A M
E V E L O H D A L E N U G D T S S N N A
E E L L N O H H L A B N A R E T I M G N
T R I Y D R I I N P G O I R L E D A E H
N L A W O E G G K R A E U A E N E R L A
E Y S O N D H H A F K R J L L D I K E T
W H T O U I G L U M T X K P E P T E S T
Y I R D W T A I N B W H B L N V A T P A
O L E E Q C T N H F H Y F W A C A R E N
R L E L Z H E E P U B V G D F K I R K L
K S T I S U N S E T A N D V I N E H D L
```

FUN FACTS: After the release of the song *The Black Dog* on *the tortured poets department* in April 2024, a south London pub called The Black Dog, rumoured to be the subject of the song, made headlines as it became swamped with Taylor Swift fans. The pub staff were delighted and seized the opportunity, offering Swift-themed burgers and cocktails and hosting album singalongs.

The image of the black dog has been used as a metaphor for mental illness, and particularly depression, in everything from classical mythology through medieval folklore up to modern day. It was used by Roman poets Horace (c. 40BC) and Appollonius (c. 1st century AD), as well as Sir Winston Churchill, who famously used it to describe his darker moods. For many people, this metaphor describes a state of depression characterized by sadness or a weakness of will.

Clara Bow, who is referenced on a different track on the album, had a black dog that she wrote a three-page eulogy for when he died.

CONNECT THE DOTS

CONNECT THE DOTS TO REVEAL TAYLOR'S FAVORITE ANIMAL, THEN COLOR THEM IN AND GIVE THEM A NAME

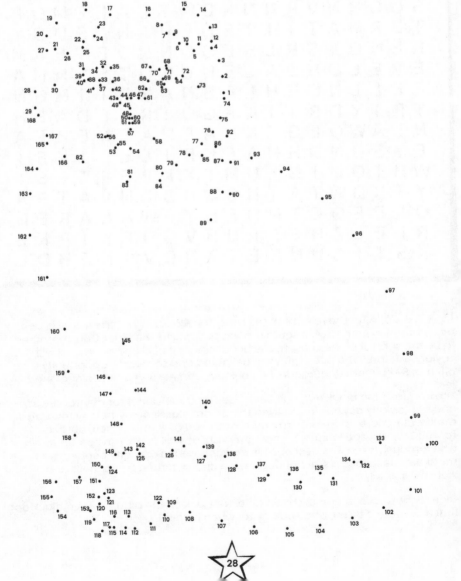

MISS AMERICANA

TAYLOR SWIFT'S AUTOBIOGRAPHICAL DOCUMENTARY WAS RELEASED IN 2020

The film provides a peek into Taylor's life, including many shots set in Electric Lady Studios in New York City. Can you mark the other American states and cities mentioned in Taylor's songs on this map?

Florida

Georgia

Los Angeles

Las Vegas

New York

Pennsylvania

Rhode Island

St. Louis

Tennessee

Texas

Tupelo

SUDOKLU

USE THE KEY ON THE OPPOSITE PAGE TO FILL OUT THE MISSING BOXES AND UNLOCK A SUDOKU PUZZLE

A				8		E		B
	B	2			9	F	6	
5	8			I				
	3	4	G					
	E		F	7	I		C	
					4	G	1	
				3			A	D
	D	C	4			1	F	
H		E		2				9

KEY

A = Rhymes with 'tour'.

B = The number of letters in the word which describes Taylor's original genre of music.

C = The second digit of Taylor's lucky number.

D = The second digit of the age Taylor sings about feeling on her *Red* album.

E = When Taylor moves through crowds of fans with outstretched hands she'll often give them a high ____.

F = Number of letters in the title of the first album Taylor released in 2020, which is a word for traditional customs, tales, sayings, dances, or art forms preserved among a people. This album had a sister album released later in the year called *evermore*.

G = The missing number in album title 198_.

H = Several of Taylor's albums, including *Speak Now*, *Red*, *1989*, *reputation*, and *Lover* debuted at number ___ on the Billboard 200 chart.

I = The *Washington Post* reported that nearly 200 Taylor Swift fans in Argentina camped out for half a year (____ months) outside River Plate Stadium, taking turns to sleep in tents there each night to hold their spots in the queue, with the goal of securing pole position the day of the *Eras* show.

ALIBIS

....

SOME BRAND-NEW TIRES WERE STOLEN FROM THE CAR MECHANIC LAST TUESDAY NIGHT. AN INVESTIGATION IS UNDERWAY TO FIND THE THIEF

....

There are three suspects but each of them has an alibi. Where do they say they were when the crime took place, and how inebriated were each of them at the time? Each say they were alone and each drank a different number of glasses of wine.

1   Este was seen at Olive Garden.

2.   Athena didn't go to the wine bar.

3.   The person who drank the fewest glasses of wine says they were in their fishing boat.

4.   The person who drank the most says they spent the night at the wine bar.

Rules: Each item in each category can be matched to one (and only one) other item in each different category. Once you have deduced one piece of information, you can tick that box and therefore rule out the other options in that category. For example, if you know that one character has drunk two glasses of wine, you could tick the box that matches their name to two glasses of wine and put a cross in the box that shows them drinking three or four glasses, as you know they have not drunk this number. Knowing this information will help you work out what the other characters might be drinking. Using the clues and following the logic, complete the grid and find all the answers!

		Location			# glasses of wine		
		Olive garden	Wine bar	Fishing boat	2	3	4
Character	Athena						
Character	Este's husband						
Character	Este						
# glasses of wine	2						
# glasses of wine	3						
# glasses of wine	4						

EMOJI MOJO

....

MATCH THE EMOJIS TO THE SONG

....

 by

 @

 of my

34

Bejeweled

Picture To Burn

Dancing With Our Hands Tied

Bad Blood

mirrorball

King Of My Heart

Back To December

Girl At Home

Death By A Thousand Cuts

Bye Bye Baby

Breathe

The Black Dog

The Archer

FUN FACT CRYPTOGRAM

USE THE CODE BELOW TO REVEAL AN ENCRYPTED FUN FACT ABOUT TAYLOR

Some of the letters have been filled in for you. Work out the code by considering the placement of the letters you already know, revealing a hidden message. Use the key below to track which letters are linked to each number.

A	B	C	D	E	F	G	H	I	J	K	L	M
13						19		21				
N	O	P	Q	R	S	T	U	V	W	X	Y	Z
				6								

```
   _  A  _  _  _  R        _  _  A  _  _  R  _  _      _  _  A  _  _
   24 13 12 25 7  6        18 17 13 24 11 6  17 22     2  25 13 15 17


_  _  _  _  _  _     A  _  _     R  _  A  _     R  _  _  _  _  _  _  _   '
25 26 16 17 25 12    13 8  22    6  12 13 8     6  17 12 8  7  25 22 4


      _  A  _  _     _  A  _  G  _  _  _  R     J  A  _  _  _
      2  13 2  12    22 13 11 19 20 24 17 6     21 13 23 17 4


R  _  _  _  _  _  _  _     _  A  _  _  _  G     _  _  _     _  _  R  _
6  17 12 8  7  25 22 4     4  13 12 26 8  19    24 20 17    9  7  6  22


"  G  _  R  G  _  _  _  _  "     _  _  R     _  _  _     _  _  R  _  _
   19 7  6  19 17 7  11 4        18 7  6     24 20 17    18 26 6  4  24


_  _  _  _     _  _     _  _  _     _  _  _  G     G  _  R  G  _  _  _  _
25 26 8  17    7  18    24 20 17    4  7  8  19    19 7  6  19 17 7  11 4


_  _     _  _  _     A  _  _  _  _     R  _  _  _  _  A  _  _  _  _  _  _  .
7  8     24 20 17    13 25 2  11 23    6  17 14 11 24 13 24 26 7  8
```

OUT OF THE WOODS

HELP TAYLOR FIND HER WAY OUT OF THE WOODS, AVOIDING THE WOLVES AS SHE GOES!

SPELLING VAULT

SPELLING IS FUN!

Join Taylor in her love of words and find as many as you can using the central letter. Each word must have a minimum of four letters and letters can be used more than once. For bonus points, find the Taylor related word from the vault which uses all the letters!

4-letter words:

5-letter words:

6-letter words:

8-letter word:

QUICK TRIVIA QUIZ

 1.   Which famous singer was Taylor named after?

 2.   What song did Taylor sing in front of 20,000 people at a
     Philadelphia 76ers NBA Finals game when she was 12 years old?

 3.   Which record executive talent spotted Taylor when she sang at
     the Bluebird Café in Nashville alongside Liz Rose when she was
     fifteen? (Months later, when he founded Big Machine Records, he
     signed her to her first record deal, which was 13 years long. In
     2019, this executive sold Big Machine Records to another record
     executive, Scooter Braun, for $330 million, becoming the owner
     of all the masters, music videos, and artworks copyrighted by
     Big Machine, including those of Taylor's first six studio albums.
     Big Machine and Taylor became embroiled in a series of
     disagreements and Taylor revealed that the label blocked her
     from performing some of her songs. In response to the fall out,
     Taylor announced that she would re-record the six albums so
     that she could own the masters herself. Songs such as *my tears
     ricochet* are understood to be about this fall out.)

 4.   In 2014 Taylor wore a yellow shirt with three words on it that
     sent the internet wild. It was in response to a post that went
     viral on the internet of someone posting a picture of Taylor
     claiming that it was of a girl called Becky who had died from
     snorting marijuana, cautioning others not to do marijuana.
     What did Taylor's t-shirt say?

 5.   In the video about the making of the song *Call It What You Want*,
     Taylor flashes her necklace at the camera when she's singing the
     line about wanting to wear her lover's initial on a chain around
     her neck. What is the initial on her necklace?

6. What film did Taylor audition for, which involved acting out dying in Eddie Redmayne's arms, which, much to her embarrassment, she had to do with her teeth painted brown?

7. What does the t-shirt Taylor wore at the start of the music video for the song *22* say? When Taylor has posted on social media with this phrase, the Swifties have come to recognise it as a sign that she has in fact been very busy working on something that will be made public soon.

8. What word did fans spot on the cover artwork for *folklore*, prompting speculation that another album might be coming to form a trilogy with *folklore* and *evermore*? Taylor cleared up on *Jimmy Kimmel Live!* that in fact the word's appearance on the artwork was a simple mistake and just a code word used for *folklore* before the album was announced.

FUN FACT: When Taylor was nine, her family moved from their eleven-acre Christmas tree farm in Montgomery County, Pennsylvania to Wyomissing, Pennysylvania, where she soon joined the Berks County Youth Theatre Academy and entered karaoke competitions every week. During this time Taylor had an acting coach who believed in her so much he rented a space in a local mall so Taylor could perform country songs to karaoke backing tracks. When Taylor was eleven years old she spent her spring break driving around Nashville with her mom – and little brother in the back seat – visiting the offices of twenty record companies to give out copies of Taylor's demo tape. One record executive advised her to stop recording covers of other people's songs and instead write her own music.

WILD JOY

Write the answer to each question in the corresponding row or column on the crossword below.

ACROSS

4. In *I Know Places*, what type of bird does Taylor see circling amongst black clouds? Bonus clue: This creature has lent its name to a news outlet which has compared Taylor to a champion tennis player or a wizened clockmaker.

5. In *Gorgeous*, what animal does Taylor say she'll come home to? Bonus clue: this is reported to be her favorite animal.

7. In *The Archer*, alongside the king's men, which of the king's animals were unable to put Taylor back together again? Bonus clue: a couple of these creatures helped Taylor get to the 2009 VMAs by pulling her carriage.

9. In *Daylight*, what type of animal might the subject of the song have run with? Bonus clue: in the music video for *Out of the Woods* Taylor runs away from a pack of these.

10. What type of animal does Taylor compare her tattooed sleeping muse to in the song *the tortured poets department*? Bonus clue: when people refer to a _____ boyfriend (a popular term on platforms like TikTok), they are referring to partners who are extremely loyal, excitable, and devoted (two words).

12. In *Innocent*, Taylor alludes to catching which type of insect during childhood? Bonus clue: this is also the title of a song by Owl City, whose lead singer Adam Young is widely understood to be the inspiration for Taylor's song *Enchanted*.

14. In *Better Than Revenge*, Taylor sings about what insect being attracted to a flame? Bonus clue: this is the same type of insect as the Common Swift.

15. In *the last great american dynasty*, what type of pet was stolen by Rebekah Harkness and dyed green? Bonus clue: apparently, Rebekah actually dyed her neighbor's cat but Taylor changed it to a different animal in her song, perhaps because she couldn't bear the idea of a cat being dyed!

16. In *You Need To Calm Down*, Taylor says which kind of animal, alongside stones, never broke her bones? Bonus clue: this animal was one of the key symbols of the *reputation* era.

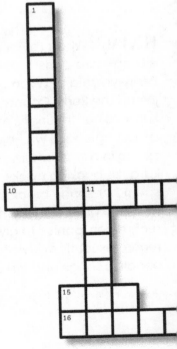

DOWN

1. In the song *Slut!,* what color pink is referred to? Bonus clue: plastic versions of these birds live on Laverne Cox's lawn in the *You Need To Calm Down* music video.

2. What insect do Taylor and the subject of the song *I'm Only Me When I'm With You* sometimes listen to instead of talking? Bonus clue: this is also the name of a sport that Taylor confused with rugby on the UK's *Graham Norton Show.*

3. What type of insect does Taylor feel in her stomach in *Everything Has Changed*? Bonus clue: she wore stilettos with these perched on the back of them at the iHeartRadio Music Awards in 2019.

6. In *You're Losing Me*, what animal does Taylor compare herself to, saying she is getting tired of continually rising from ashes? Bonus clue: according to legend there is only one of these living in the world at any time.

8. In *mad woman*, what animal is poked until their claws come out? Bonus clue: on New Year's Eve 2020 Taylor posted a photo on Instagram of herself dressed as this animal.

11. What type of magical animal does Taylor say she had the time of her life fighting in the song *Long Live*? Bonus clue: several of these creatures can be spotted flying around her castle at the end of the *Bejeweled* music video.

13. In *loml* what did the coward claim to be? Bonus clue: in *The Wizard of Oz*, there is a famous character who is this type of animal who goes with Dorothy to ask the Wizard of Oz to grant him the courage he lacks.

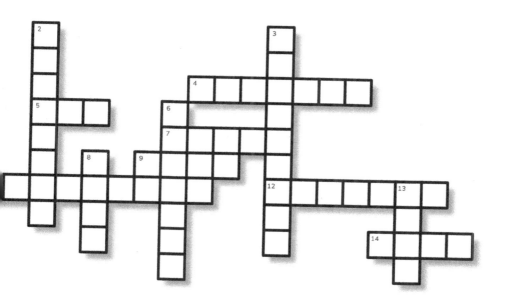

43

FOR A MONTH

MATCH THE MONTH TO THE SONG IT IS MENTIONED IN

Lover

Fortnight

High Infidelity

You All Over Me

Last Kiss

Tim McGraw

Innocent

Call It What You Want

champagne problems

Out Of The Woods

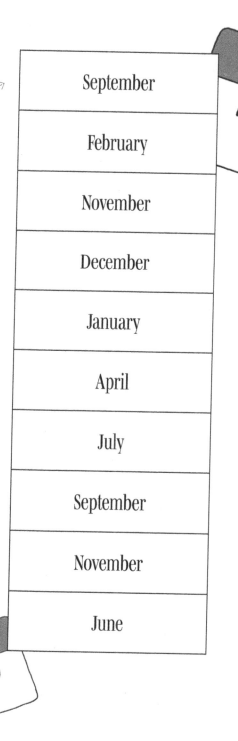

| September |
| February |
| November |
| December |
| January |
| April |
| July |
| September |
| November |
| June |

WHEN THE CLAWS COME OUT

......

TAYLOR HAS SAID THERE'S NOTHING SHE LIKES BETTER THAN REVENGE ...

......

Find terms from her battle cries in the wordsearch on the opposite page. There's also a secret word to find!

armor	dead	pitchforks
arson	desert	poison
axe	double crossed	revenge
battle	dying	rifle
bomb	flames	robbers
bullet	gun	shoot
burn	gunfight	shotgun
cage	hatchet	stones
cannonball	kill	swords
claws	killer	thief
crash	knives	war
cuts	matches	warpath
daggers	missile	wildfire
dangerous	noose	wrecking ball

```
R E V E N G E P Z C R A S H E Z Z Q P M Q B D R
S O M G P D E S E R T R K G I Z E Z S B H X K A
E S T D K Q C E S K E P W A R P A T H Z H Q A B
M H Z C K R B F C N A Y X L U W O W B M O M R O
A O W T I K C V A R M O R F K P C V O F W A M Y
C O G D A N G E R O U S H C O S Q S R A K T A T
R T C M M S J G V N D S T O N E S H I X A C D H
W C G U N F I G H T W D Y I N G F S F E R H A I
R M P P O I S O N E W I L D F I R E L A M E G E
T M H L G F W R E C K I N G B A L L E D A S G F
B I G Q G W I P E J G U N C A G E G K X E S E J
K S S M C W W P O Z B N A R S O N A F U X K R U
A S I X Q L A Z C X U O T I B B A T T L E X S X
R I L F E K R J N L R E X N A S H O T G U N A D
M L C L F L Q E J Z N F M T P P T I F J V O E E
A E D O U B L E C R O S S E D I M V P H E O C A
W O R D S W Y T B U L L E T D I T A C X N S G D
G P S F W K I L L E R G P P S W K C H Z S E D Y
O G Y L Q B P Y T R P C J I R L Z F H P H O L Y
Z F C A B O M B C J M B G K B G D C X F K I L L
R Q L M Y E A I H B C G X S N Q L D O J O F R Q
U H A E D H A T C H E T Q I P I J S X N X R F F
Q T W S G A J P D K A R M A J Z V A Q S R X K B
O S S M K S R N T D Y Y R R O B B E R S Z A P S
G G F X W V P V X P C Y N Y M W S E S E P J U E
```

A SICK BEAT

RANK THESE TAYLOR SWIFT SONGS IN ORDER OF BEATS PER MINUTE – THE SPEED OF THE SONG

willow

Shake It Off

Karma

the last great american dynasty

cardigan

1

2

3

4

5

Fastest

Slowest

MUSIC IN MY MIND

THESE QUESTIONS ARE FOR THE REAL MUSIC EXPERTS OUT THERE

Answer these music trivia questions to reveal the secret code by placing the letter answers in order in the boxes below.

1. What is the first letter of the word which describes the musical term for when a collection of songs are played one after another as a single piece of music, as Taylor frequently does in her shows?

2. What key are the songs *Don't Blame Me* and *this is me trying* in?

3. What is the first letter of the single-reed woodwind instrument that plays the riff in the song *False God* and features on many other of Taylor's songs?

4. Most of Taylor's songs are written in 4/4. This is an example of a _____ signature? Put the first letter of this word in the last box.

5. Taylor is often seen playing a red Gibson Les Paul. What type of guitar is this? Put the first letter in the 5th box.

6. The first letter of the musical term for a line or phrase that is repeated in a song, often shorter than the chorus.

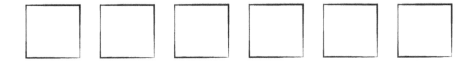

49

TEACH SOME LESSONS

TAYLOR EXCELLED ACADEMICALLY BUT HAS OFTEN TALKED ABOUT HOW SHE'S STILL HAUNTED BY INSECURITIES BORN FROM FEELING UNCOOL AT SCHOOL

Fortunately, she made some good friends, like Abigail, who she sat next to in English class on the first day in freshman year and who quickly became her best friend. Abigail has featured in several of Taylor's music videos, including for the song *Fifteen*, which even references Abigail by name. Use the code to find all the words related to school days that may trigger these memories, both happy and hard.

1	2	3	4	5	6	7	8	9	10	11	12	13
					r					o	h	
14	15	16	17	18	19	20	21	22	23	24	25	26
								m				e

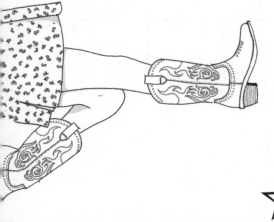

FOR THE SWIFTIES

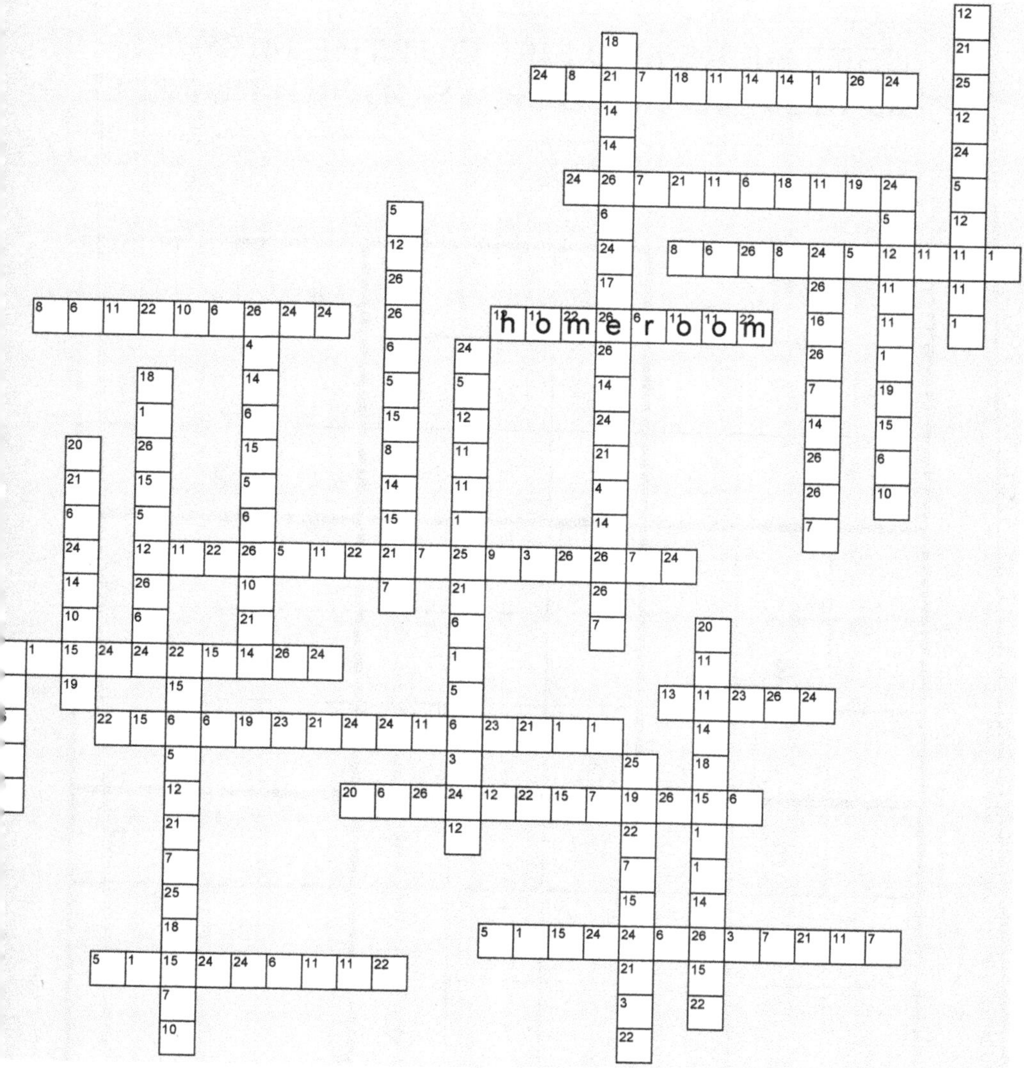

SUDOKLU

USE THE KEY TO FILL OUT THE MISSING
BOXES AND UNLOCK A SUDOKU PUZZLE

			1			8		
	E			A	B			G
5		D	H				3	
G				5	1	4		
	9						2	
		6	2	I				A
	5				7	C		8
C			B	8			7	
		F			6			

KEY

....

A = The name of a song on the album that is set in Pennsylvania and is about childhood.

B = Which track number on Taylor's albums is known to be a really honest, emotional, vulnerable and personal song?

C = The number of albums Braun and then Shamrock Holdings purchased, which Taylor determined to re-record.

D = The number referenced in the name of the first song on the *folklore* album.

E = The number of letters in the first name of Taylor's cat, who is named after a character on *Grey's Anatomy*, Dr _____ Grey, played by Ellen Pompeo.

F = Number of letters in the title of a song about a cruel critic, which won her a Grammy in 2012.

G = At what time in the morning does Taylor feel like she just lost a friend in the song *Breathe*?

H = In Taylor's song *Back To December*, in which month (from 1-12) did the person she's singing about see her cry for the first time?

I = Taylor first became a billionaire in October 202_. It was declared by *Forbes* the next year.

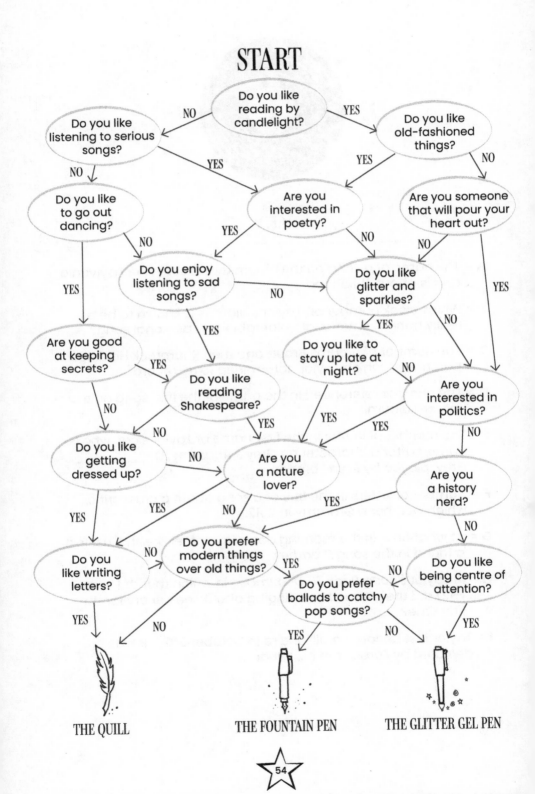

START

Do you like reading by candlelight?

Do you like listening to serious songs?

Do you like old-fashioned things?

Do you like to go out dancing?

Are you interested in poetry?

Are you someone that will pour your heart out?

Do you enjoy listening to sad songs?

Do you like glitter and sparkles?

Are you good at keeping secrets?

Do you like to stay up late at night?

Do you like reading Shakespeare?

Are you interested in politics?

Do you like getting dressed up?

Are you a nature lover?

Are you a history nerd?

Do you like writing letters?

Do you prefer modern things over old things?

Do you prefer ballads to catchy pop songs?

Do you like being centre of attention?

THE QUILL

THE FOUNTAIN PEN

THE GLITTER GEL PEN

PEN-SONALITY TEST

TAYLOR REVEALED THAT SHE CATEGORIZES HER SONGS INTO THREE DIFFERENT PEN TYPES: THE QUILL, THE FOUNTAIN PEN AND THE GLITTER GEL PEN

Take the quiz to the left to find out which pen you are!

THE QUILL

You are an old soul and lover of all things old-fashioned. You are known for having classic taste and a curious mind. At the weekends you could be found with your head in a book, and you like reading poetry and novels. You love wearing vintage clothes and spending cosy nights in, preferring to adventure in your imagination.

THE FOUNTAIN PEN

You are an open and generous person who likes to talk to others and share your experiences. Your friends value you for your insights and you like to keep up-to-date with what is happening in the world. You always stand up for what you believe in and care deeply about social issues.

THE GLITTER GEL PEN

You are often described as the life and soul of the party and enjoy getting dressed up and being glamorous. You are fun-loving and adventure-seeking, and like being around other people. You are a night owl and like to dance around your room when no one is looking – and when they are!

LOVE TRIANGLE

THE SCHOOL GYM IS A BLUR OF STUDENTS DANCING

Too crowded for some and just right for others. The disco ball reflects light across the tangle of bouncing bodies and it's hard to tell who is who in the crowd, some only distinguishable by their signature pieces of clothing. James' eyes are on Betty, Augustine's eyes are on James, and Betty is on the far side of the gym. How many different people do each of these characters wind up dancing with and what signature items of clothing are they wearing? Each has a different signature item of clothing and each danced with a different number of people.

1. James is wearing Levi's.

2. Betty isn't wearing a sweatshirt.

3. The person who danced with the fewest people is wearing Levi's.

4. The person wearing a sweatshirt danced with 2 people.

Rules: Each item of the category is matched to one (and only one) other item in each different category. Once you have deduced one piece of information, you can tick that box and therefore rule out the other options in that category, placing a cross in those boxes. For example, if you know that one character is wearing Levi's, you could tick the box that matches their name to Levi's and put a cross in the box that shows them wearing the other items of clothing, as you know they are not wearing those. Knowing this information will help you work out what the other characters might be wearing. Using the clues and following the logic, complete the grid and find all the answers!

		Clothing			# dances		
		Cardigan	Levi's	Sweatshirt	3	2	1
Character	James						
Character	Augustine						
Character	Betty						
# dances	3						
# dances	2						
# dances	1						

57

FUN FACT CRYPTOGRAM

USE THE CODE BELOW TO REVEAL AN ENCRYPTED FUN FACT ABOUT TAYLOR

Some of the letters have been filled in for you. Work out the code by considering the placement of the letters you already know, revealing a hidden message. Use the key below to track which letters are linked to each number.

A	B	C	D	E	F	G	H	I	J	K	L	M
						25						

N	O	P	Q	R	S	T	U	V	W	X	Y	Z
				10			26				19	

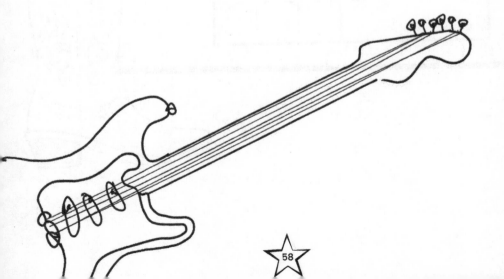

— —   2 0 1 0   — —   2 0   Y __ __ R __   — — — ,
4 18   16 15   19 17 16 10 24   6 22 2

— — Y — — R   — — —   —   G R __ __ __ Y   — — R
15 16 19 22 6 10   11 6 18   16   25 10 16 7 7 19   1 6 10

— — — U __   — —   — — —   Y __ __ R   — — R
16 22 3 26 7   6 1   15 5 17   19 17 16 10   1 6 10

— — — R — — — — ,   — — — — — G   __ __ R   — — —
1 17 16 10 22 17 24 24   7 16 20 4 18 25   5 17 10   15 5 17

Y __ U __ G — — —   — — R — — —   — —   R — — — — — —
9 6 26 18 25 17 24 15   13 17 10 24 6 18   15 6   10 17 21 17 4 23 17

— — —   — — — R __ .
15 5 17   16 11 16 10 2

LOOK WHAT YOU MADE ME DUET

MATCH THE TAYLOR SWIFT SONGS TO THE FEATURED COLLABORATOR

A. *Bad Blood (Remix)*

B. *Both Of Us*

C. *Breathe*

D. *Castles Crumbling*

E. *coney island*

F. *Electric Touch*

G. *Everything Has Changed*

H. *exile*

I. *Florida!!!*

J. *Fortnight*

K. *I Bet You Think About Me*

L. *I Don't Wanna Live Forever*

M. *Karma (Remix)*

N. *Lover (Remix)*

O. *ME!*

P. *no body, no crime*

Q. *Nothing New*

R. *Safe & Sound*

S. *Snow On The Beach*

T. *Soon You'll Get Better*

U. *That's When*

V. *The Last Time*

W. *You All Over Me*

Ice Spice

B.o.B

Ed Sheeran

Kendrick Lamar

V Gary Lightbody

Lana Del Rey

Colbie Caillat

The Civil Wars

Maren Morris

Hayley Williams

Phoebe Bridgers

Shawn Mendes

The National

Chris Stapleton

Fall Out Boy

HAIM

The Chicks

Bon Iver

Brendon Urie

Florence + the Machine

Keith Urban

Post Malone

ZAYN

LOVE STORIES

....

OUR GIRL LOVES LOVE!
AND SHE LOVES TO SING ABOUT IT TOO

....

Pick out the different ways she describes love and lovers in the wordsearch on the opposite page.

a game

a masterpiece

alive

bad

burning

chemistry

crooked

cruel

delicate

drug

electric

faithless

fly

frozen

golden

good

gravity

great

legendary

like the colors in autumn

like white wine

magnetic

mansion with a view

maroon

mine

my drug

my homeland

passionate

rare

reckless

red

treacherous

trouble

```
O A P Y T M Y P A S S I O N A T E O O M X L M X N
O P Q B M Y H O M E L A N D A K V K Y D S B R E Z
L C Y P V L F O I V E R M C L I Z A B J R M W A M
G I G B F O F R L X U C H I I V Q F U X K U S H Y
F G K V V C T R O U B L E A V C R G R Q K N G H D
S I V E S J F I D Z M R O L E R D M N E P M F N R
T Q R A T A O A V N E R M E X O F A I Q O A F Z U
R C M M P H V A X E X N P G F O M G N V X N X J G
Y A M A S T E R P I E C E E J K E N G A L S X W P
I G V S J E X C X D C E G N Q E U E F X R I G Y X
G L R B Y A K M O W Y T G D W D Q T F B C O O M Q
M I K E N H G F C L C P D A M F S I W R Q N A X V
G K C E A O Y A Y Z O H W R K S C C I N X W Q F C
R E P H H T J P M T X R U Y C V P Y P D E I U E I
A W U U E M I N E E R Q S E O S W J R P L T Y W H
V H M K S M B N M C H E D I G E I N A B E H C U V
I I A I F H I G Z N D J A O N O L Z R V C A R G U
T T R R A H B S J O Z F A C V A L V E M T V J O C
Y E O V I L A F T W B Z L A H R U D C D R I X O V
Y W O V T H D O I R H E D Y L E Z T E J I E F D L
F I N N H H K O S H Y F R C F U R G U N C W X Z K
W N D E L I C A T E V I N F Z A P O O M J H Z U S
T E R N E C R U E L Y Y M U I J I R U J N W X D S
O H W U S A L K I N J V R E C K L E S S Y V E F
L L B T S I K Z C H N W R Q L W A D P V Z Y Y T F
```

FLASHING LIGHTS

HELP TAYLOR DODGE THE PAPARAZZI AS SHE HIDES UNDER AN UMBRELLA

FUN FACT: The song *epiphany* was partly inspired by Taylor's paternal grandfather Dean, who fought at the Battle of Guadalcanal, an American military campaign against the Empire of Japan, in the Second World War. Taylor told *Vogue* that he *'never talked about it, not with his sons, not with his wife. Nobody got to hear what happened there. So I tried to imagine what would happen in order to make you never be able to speak about something. I realized that there are people right now taking a 20-minute break between shifts at a hospital who are having this trauma happen to them that they will probably never want to speak about. I just thought, this is an opportunity to maybe tell those stories.'*

A picture of Dean appears in the *cardigan* music video, the first song on the *folklore* album. The song *epiphany* is placed at number 13 on the *folklore* album. The song *marjorie*, which is about Taylor's maternal grandmother, is placed at number 13 on *folklore's* sister album, *evermore*. So both grandparents have a song linked to Taylor's lucky number!

COME IN WITH THE RAIN

Write the answer to each question in the corresponding row or column on the crossword below.

ACROSS

3. In what song on Taylor's *Fearless* album does she sing about not being able to help wanting to kiss her muse in the rain?

6. In what song on Taylor's debut album does she sing about being left outside in the rain like a type of coin?

7. In what song on Taylor's *the tortured poets department* album does she sing that when the subject of the song has the sky rain fire upon them, and when they're no longer in favor, that she'll tell them how she's also been there and that none of it matters?

9. In what song on *Speak Now* does Taylor say that the subject of the song paints her a blue sky and then turns it to rain?

10. In what song on *folklore* does Taylor sing that it is always going to rain if the subject of the song is with her?

12. In what song on *Midnights* does Taylor describe herself as rain at midnight?

14. In what song on Taylor's debut album does she sing that it's a shame to have it rain at the end of a perfect day?

15. In what song on Taylor's *the tortured poets department* album does Taylor sing that she doesn't understand why the subject of her song doesn't miss her in the shower and recall how her body was shaking from the rain?

16. In what song on *Speak Now* does Taylor remember the smell of rain as it hits the pavement?

17. In what song on *Lover* does Taylor ask to be shown a grey sky and a rainy cab drive?

18. In what song on *Speak Now* does Taylor compare the way her love moves to a full-blown storm, asking them to drop everything and meet her in the pelting rain?

DOWN

1. In what song on *evermore* does Taylor sing that her eyes drip acid rain onto a pillow?

2. In what song on *Red* does Taylor sing that all she knows is driving rain and that everything is different now?

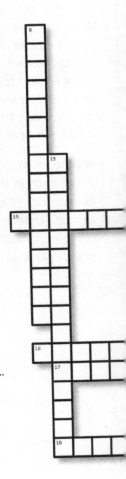

FOR THE SWIFTIES

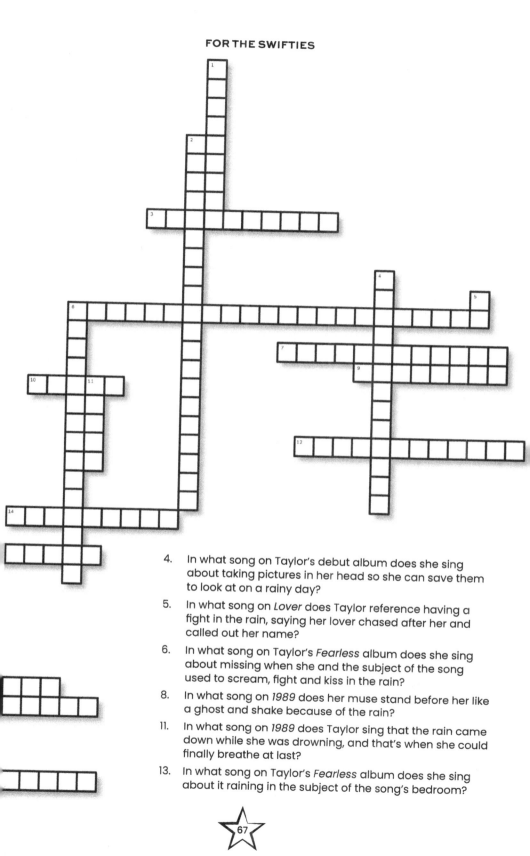

4. In what song on Taylor's debut album does she sing about taking pictures in her head so she can save them to look at on a rainy day?

5. In what song on *Lover* does Taylor reference having a fight in the rain, saying her lover chased after her and called out her name?

6. In what song on Taylor's *Fearless* album does she sing about missing when she and the subject of the song used to scream, fight and kiss in the rain?

8. In what song on *1989* does her muse stand before her like a ghost and shake because of the rain?

11. In what song on *1989* does Taylor sing that the rain came down while she was drowning, and that's when she could finally breathe at last?

13. In what song on Taylor's *Fearless* album does she sing about it raining in the subject of the song's bedroom?

THE ERAS TOUR QUIZ

1. Seismic activity equivalent to what magnitude of earthquake did fans cause dancing to *Shake It Off* during the Seattle show of the Eras Tour on July 23rd 2023?

   a. 1.2   b. 1.8   c. 2.3

2. What is the name of the choreographer for the Eras Tour?

   a. Parris Goebel   b. Mandy Moore   c. JaQuel Knight

3. When Eras Tour tickets first went on sale in November 2022 on Ticketmaster, the site crashed due to the extraordinarily high demand. 3.5 million people had pre-registered for Taylor's Verified Fan sale, which was the largest sale in history and 14 million accounts tried to access the site. How many stadium shows would Taylor have to play to meet the demand on the site that day?

   a. A stadium show every single night for the next six months

   b. A stadium show every single night for the next 2.5 years

   c. A stadium show every single night for the next 25 years

4. The Eras Tour became the first tour to surpass $............ in revenue, making it the highest-grossing tour ever to exist. This surpassed Elton John as the previous record holder.

   a. $500 million   b. $800 million   c. $1 billion

5. Towards the end of the first US leg of the Eras Tour, Taylor reportedly gave over $55 million in bonuses to everyone working on the tour. How much did each truck driver on the tour reportedly receive as a bonus?

   a. $10,000   b. $100,000   c. $1,000,000

6. How many fans attended the opening night of the Eras Tour in Glendale, Arizona, breaking the record for the most attended concert by a female artist in the US?

   a. 69,000   b. 75,000   c. 81,000

7. Which country filed the 'Taylor Swift Law', penalizing those reselling tickets with fines up to 100 times the original ticket price?

   a. Brazil   b. Japan   c. Italy

8. How long is the movie *Taylor Swift: The Eras Tour*?

   a. 3 hours and 15 minutes

   b. 2 hours 48 minutes

   c. 1 hour 51 minutes

9. Where was the movie *Taylor Swift: The Eras Tour* recorded? It was recorded over three shows with a budget of $10–20 million.

    a. Los Angeles   b. Singapore   c. Florida

10. During which song on the Eras Tour does Taylor give one lucky audience member her hat at each show?

    a. *Style*   b. *22*   c. *We Are Never Getting Back Together*

11. The Enchanted dress Taylor wore in the Speak Now portion of the Eras Tour while performing her second show in Arizona was custom-made Zuhair Murad couture. How many meters of tulle and how many hours of atelier handwork did it take to create?

    a. 13 meters and 130 hours

    b. 22 meters and 202 hours

    c. 50 meters and 350 hours

12. Nicole + Felicia Couture created multiple *Enchanted* ball gowns for Taylor to wear on tour, including a gold one with 200,000 sequins and crystals on it. How many hours did the blue *Enchanted* gown reportedly take to complete? Taylor wore this during the Eras Tour in L.A. when she announced *1989* (*Taylor's Version*).

    a. 500   b. 2,100   c. 10,300

13. What does Taylor reportedly hide in to get behind the stage without concert goers spotting her?

    a. A suitcase   b. A trash can   c. A janitor cart

FUN FACTS: The guitar covered in silver rhinestones that Taylor uses during the *Fearless* portion of the concert, which matches the guitar she used during the *Fearless* tour in 2009, was decorated by her parents using, as Taylor put it on her Instagram, "super glue and a free afternoon."

Taylor's workout routine for the Eras Tour reportedly included singing the full set list of songs – over 40 of them – while running and walking on a treadmill every day, running for fast songs and jogging or walking for slower ones.

In a story for GlobeNewswire, QuestionPro estimated that the Eras Tour will generate $5 billion in economic impact in the US alone, more than the gross domestic product of 50 countries.

SNAKES AND STONES

CONNECT THE SNAKE'S HEAD AND TAIL TO COMPLETE ITS BODY

The numbers around the outside of the grid tell you how many pieces of snake are to be placed in each row and column. Within each square the snake can either move in a straight line or turn at a 90-degree angle.

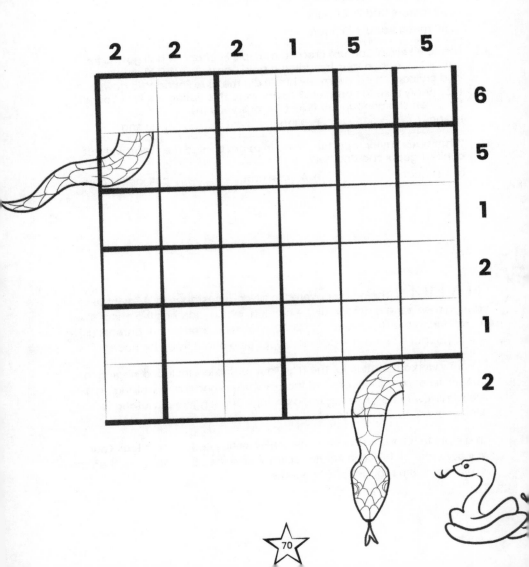

SPELLING VAULT

SPELLING IS FUN!

Join Taylor in her love of words and find as many as you can using the central letter. Each word must have a minimum of four letters and letters can be used more than once. For bonus points, find the Taylor Swift nickname from the vault that uses all the letters!

4-letter words:

5-letter words:

6-letter words:

7-letter words:

8-letter words:

SINGONYMS

WHICH TAYLOR SWIFT SONG TITLES ARE HIDDEN IN THESE SYNONYMS?

1. So Long Infant

2. Communicate Immediately

3. Final Smooch

4. Sacred Earth

5. Melancholy Pretty Grievous

6. Start Over

7. The Instant I Realised

8. Female In The House

9. Unmarked Area

10. Label It As You Wish

11. I Consigned To Oblivion That You Are Extant

12. Big Smoke Lad

13. Impossible To Be In Contact With

MASTERMINDS

FOR EACH MASTER, ANSWER THESE QUIZ QUESTIONS TO FIND CODE WORDS, THEN GUESS WHAT THE CODE WORDS HAVE IN COMMON

MASTER 1

1. Forbidden fruit, which Taylor uses as a prop in her *Blank Space* music video.

2. A word you would say to greet a guest as they enter your home. Taylor often uses it at the start of a performance while on tour, such as '____ to the Eras tour!'

3. A well-known phrase from the United States Declaration of Independence is 'Life, ____, and the pursuit of Happiness'.

4. Taylor Swift was which magazine's Person of the Year in 2023? Make it plural and you've got your clue.

5. Song on *evermore* in which Taylor sings about sitting on a bench, wondering where her baby went.

MASTER 2

1. *Hey* ___ , song on Taylor's second album. Make it plural and you've got your clue.

2. First name of an English actor who played Loki in *Thor* and reportedly dated Taylor Swift in 2016.

3. This English composer and impresario wrote the score for *Joseph and the Amazing Technicolor Dreamcoat*, which happens to have a song called *King of My Heart*, as does Taylor's *reputation* album.

4. The first name of one of the founding fathers of the USA, who features on the $100 bill.

5. A detective who is the main protagonist of the NBC procedural drama *Law & Order: Special Victims Unit*, portrayed by Mariska Hargitay.

MASTER 3

1. In the *reputation* album, what did Taylor buy just so her lover could take it off?

2. Piece of jewellery seen on the *Red (Taylor's Version)* album cover.

3. What does Taylor take a lick of and then a chunk out of in the music video *I Bet You Think About Me (Taylor's Version)*?

4. In Spring 2022, what did Taylor give to NYU's graduating class? During this commencement _____, she included several Easter eggs for her upcoming *Midnights* album.

MASTER 4

1. Taylor Swift was a guest advisor to Adam Levine on the TV show *The Voice*. What is the first word of the name of the band Adam is a lead singer in?

2. What does Taylor wake up in in *Down Bad*?

3. What kind of wine is on Taylor's t-shirt in *Maroon*?

4. Which stone fruit does Taylor use to describe her lips in *Blank Space*?

MASTER 5

1. What mix of colours is the pride flag famous for having?

2. 'All's ____ in love and war' is a proverb Taylor has adapted for *the tortured poets department*, switching 'war' for 'poetry'.

3. What common phrase to describe love from the 50s was Taylor inspired by when watching *Mad Men*? Lavender ____.

4. Which day do the lovers in *You Are In Love* have burnt toast at his place on? _____day.

MASTER 6

1. In *Picture To Burn*, what was wasted, which Taylor struck a match on?

2. What does Taylor spill in the bathtub in *Dress*?

3. What is the first word of the name of the film with *Wildest Dreams* as part of the soundtrack?

4. Despite not giving this to narcissists, apparently they love Taylor.

A ROYAL COMPETITION

WHILE HOUSE WENCH TAYLOR HAS BEEN SCRUBBING FLOORS, HER EVIL STEPSISTERS HAVE BEEN BUSY FASTENING NIPPLE TASSELS AND CONTOURING THEIR ABS WITH MUD FROM THE HOG PEN OUTSIDE TO PREPARE FOR THE UPCOMING BALL

Each stepsister will compete to win the prince's favor, and each has a different desire. Just in case it helps their chances, they all intend to leave one of their shoes behind... What do they each desire and what size shoes will they be wearing to the ball? Each has a different desire and each will be wearing a different shoe size.

1. Lady Alana doesn't want the title.

2. Lady Danielle wants the ring.

3. The person who desires the D*** has the smallest shoe size.

4. The person who has shoes bigger than Lady Alana has smaller shoes than the person who desires the title.

Rules: Each item of the category is matched to one (and only one) other item in each different category. Once you have deduced one piece of information, you can tick that box and therefore rule out the other options in that category, placing a cross in those boxes. For example, if you know that one character wants the ring, you could tick the box that matches their name to the ring and put a cross in the box that shows them wanting other things, as you know they are not wanting those. Knowing this information will help you work out what the other characters might be wanting and wearing. Using the clues and following the logic, complete the grid and find all the answers!

		Desires			Shoe size		
		The ring	The title	The D***	3	5	8
Character	Lady Danielle						
	Lady Este						
	Lady Alana						
Shoe size	3						
	5						
	8						

DESCRAMBLE

USE THE CLUES BELOW TO HELP YOU UNSCRAMBLE THESE TAYLOR SWIFT SONGS

1. A moment of sudden realization

2. The bird with the largest wingspan

3. A predication of something that will happen in the future

4. A synonym for 'stunning' or 'beautiful'

5. The perfect accessory for a dance floor to make things glitter

6. The setting for Lewis Carroll's famous children's novel based around the character Alice

7. An animal that carries mythical properties, and in more than one tradition is ridden by patron saints

8. A famous American comic strip character that you can also see in the movies

9. A tree which belongs to the family Salicaceae

10. The holiday which marks the start of the year

1. INEHPAYP

2. ETH SRSBALTAO

3. HET ECPYHOPR

4. OEGUGSRO

5. RORBRMILLA

6. DEWLNANORD

7. THIEW OESRH

8. MRNAUSPE

9. LWIOLW

10. WEN ERYAS' YDA

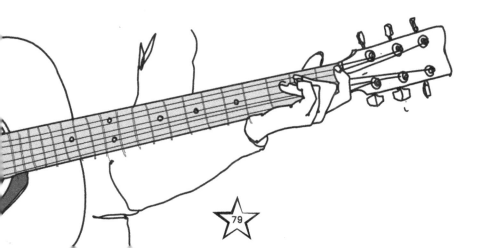

THROUGH THE GARDEN GATE

SHE'S A FORCE OF NATURE AND OFTEN SETS THE SCENE WITH IT. CAN YOU PICK THE PLANTS OUT OF THE WORD GARDEN ON THE OPPOSITE PAGE?

autumn leaves	mistletoe
branches	morning glory
bushes	petals
carnation	poppy
cedar	roots
clover	rose
daisy	seed
garden	thorns
grass	tree
hedge maze	violets
holly	weeds
ivy	willow
lavender	wisteria
lawn	woods

```
D B L Z S E E D Y Z V L C X T W W P V E G D A B G
N M T Y W N M W E E D S M C F V W W R Z B Y P R L
Z L C Y G N L P B C U J U L A W N R I P D A K A M
V A N W N P M O R N I N G G L O R Y R L R O U P F
Q V G T S S Z Y A C Q R Y P P O P P Y A L H I Q P
C E A J W D I T N L M S O V X O B C O T N O E C B
C N T H O R N S C X E W P O M A F O D Y H N W D U
I D C O U M Y N H T Z K Q Q T Z W W I L I C N S S
D E E B X I K A E C N R N G X S J W T E J O U T H
N R D K S S Z Y S Z B Z N C A T F P H V Q D Z B E
F A P I G T I K Y O E O B L E R G W A G E J K F S
B G W Z E L O R X H Y B P I L D D Z M N J W P V X
K R K E W E F G A H B H E A R N A E F X U I M M J
S A R N Z T U P M P T O C U A V Q R N P W S W Y I
N S W P D O E K S Q G L R T M I A L H D A T K H N
A S R K F E L G S L O L U U R K Y Q H X N E O P F
B C L O V E R I V X J Y Y M F X H A Q R G R I D Z
S D P E N S O F M D T Y G N K N T R E E W I V J N
E J A N O R G W L H A J Z L I F W C D V X A Y L S
Z F Q Z H D Z K Z W C K H E V V L Z A U N G A W W
M R A V M M C Z W S G Y J A S R U S I G N Q I W O
D O Z S Q Y Q X Z I I B J V K H W X S W D Q D L O
Q S H X H E D G E M A Z E E L D C H Y U T L M Q D
U E B I F L E L K M H R O S C A R N A T I O N S S
I O V G K V I O L E T S F Y N P E T A L S U D D V
```

81

FUN FACT CRYPTOGRAM

USE THE CODE BELOW TO REVEAL AN ENCRYPTED FUN FACT ABOUT TAYLOR

Some of the letters have been filled in for you. Work out the code by considering the placement of the letters you already know, revealing a hidden message. Use the key below to track which letters are linked to each number.

A	B	C	D	E	F	G	H	I	J	K	L	M
17											14	
N	O	P	Q	R	S	T	U	V	W	X	Y	Z
					1							

```
 __   __   __   __      __   A    __   L    __   __      __   A    S         __   __   __   L    __   __
 12   10   4    2       24   17   3    14   7    20      12   17   1         24   12   4    14   23   4


           __   A    __   S         __   L    __   ,        __   __   __   __   __   __   __   __
           3    4    17   20   1     7    14   16           6    7    13   15   26   24   4    20


      __   __   __   A    __   __   __   A    __      A    __   __         L    __   __   A    L
      20   4    15   17   8    20   13   17   2        17   2    16         14   7    6    17   14


      __   __   S    __   __   __   A    __          __   __   __   __   __   __        __   __   __   __   __   __
      13   26   1    8    6    8    17   2           20   7    2    2    8    4         6    20   4    13   4    20


 __   A    __   __   __   __         __   __   __         __   __         __   L    A    __         __   __   __   __   A    __   .
 24   17   26   9    10   24         10   4    20         24   7          15   14   17   3          9    26   8    24   17   20


 __   __   __         __   __   __   S    __         S    __   __   __         S    __   __         L    __   A    __   __   __   __
 24   10   4          25   8    20   1    24          1    7    2    9          1    10   4          14   4    17   20   2    4    16


 __   __         __   L    A    __         __   A    S         S    __   __   __   __   __   __   __         __   __   __   __
 24   7          15   14   17   3          12   17   1          1    8    21   15   4    2    6    4         2    7    2    4


 __   __   __         __   __   __   __   __   __         '   S         __   __   __         __   __   S    S         __   __   .
 24   10   4          20   8    6    10   4    20           1          10   8    24         22   8    1    1         13   4
```

CONNECT THE DOTS

JOIN THE DOTS TO FIND ONE OF TAYLOR'S FAVORITE ITEMS OF CLOTHING

84

GETAWAY CAR

HELP TAYLOR GET FROM THE X MARKING THE SPOT WHERE THINGS FELL APART TO FREEDOM IN HER GETAWAY CAR

IF THIS WAS A MOVIE

MATCH THE TAYLOR SWIFT SONGS TO THE FILMS THEY SOUNDTRACK

Crazier

Today Was a Fairytale

Safe & Sound

Sweeter Than Fiction

I Don't Wanna Live Forever

Beautiful Ghosts

Only the Young

Carolina

Director

Scene

Take

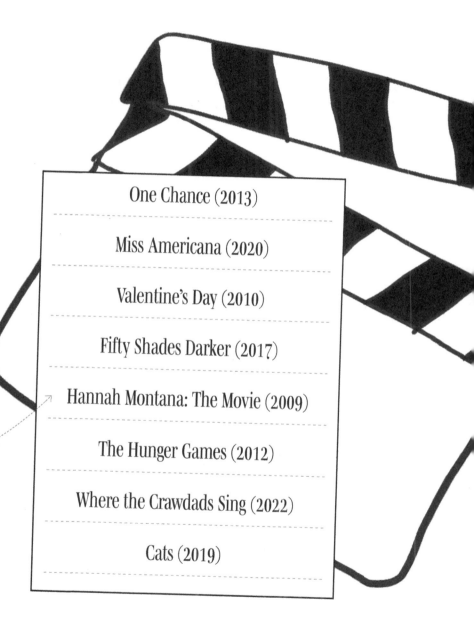

One Chance (2013)

Miss Americana (2020)

Valentine's Day (2010)

Fifty Shades Darker (2017)

Hannah Montana: The Movie (2009)

The Hunger Games (2012)

Where the Crawdads Sing (2022)

Cats (2019)

SUDOKLU

USE THE KEY TO FILL OUT THE MISSING
BOXES AND UNLOCK A SUDOKU PUZZLE

F	H	I	9					
		C		2		F	A	
			3	E				
A		6	8		B			
H								9
			H		9	D		1
				G	C			
	4	E		5		9		
					1	B	5	C

KEY

A = At the end of *Mary's Song (Oh My My My)* Taylor says she'll be 87 and you'll be 8_, and that she'll still look at you as if you were a star in the sky.

B = *Midnights* was released 202_

C = The number of letters in Taylor's maternal grandmother's name.

D = In *High Infidelity*, which month (from 1-12) does Taylor reference? She asks the listener if they really want to know where she was on the 29th of that month.

E = When DJ David Mueller sued Taylor for defamation, seeking approximately $3 million in damages, Taylor counter-sued for battery and sexual assault, seeking a symbolic $__ in damages. The jury ruled in Taylor's favor. Taylor revealed her reasoning for counter-suing was to empower other victims of sexual assault and also donated to organizations that help fund legal costs of sexual assault victims who choose to defend themselves.

F = *Reputation* was Taylor's __th album.

G = *betty* is one of how many songs on the *folklore* album about a certain set of characters in high school?

H = The second digit of the age Taylor sings about in the *Fearless* album, when if someone tells you they love you, you're going to believe them.

I = In *You Need To Calm Down*, at what time are people taking shots at Taylor like they're Patrón?

DRINKS IN THE BAR

ACROSS

Write the answer to each question in the corresponding row or column on the crossword below.

2. In the song *Gorgeous*, what drink does Taylor refer to, served on ice, right before she says the subject of the song is ruining her life by not being hers?

5. In the song *the 1*, what drink was flowing with chosen family?

6. In the song *This Is Why We Can't Have Nice Things*, what did everyone swim in a sea of?

8. In the song *The Albatross*, what is the only thing that anoints the subject of the song?

9. In the song *august*, the month slipped away like what receptacle of wine?

11. In the song *Maroon*, what type of bottle was the roommate's cheap rosé in?

12. In the song *Dress*, what does Taylor spill in the bath?

13. In the song *King Of My Heart*, what does Taylor drink out of plastic cups up on the roof?

15. In the song *Getaway Car*, Taylor says that she knew from the first one of this cocktail - traditionally made with Scotch whiskey or bourbon, sugar, and bitters, and garnished with orange peel - that she and the subject of the song were cursed.

16. In the song *Clean*, Taylor sings about how wine has done what to her dress?

DOWN

1. In the song *no body, no crime*, what type of wine does Este notice on her husband's mouth?

3. In the song *...Ready For It?*, which cocktail – traditionally made with rum, cranberry juice and grapefruit juice – does Taylor reference, right before she says that the lights are low?

4. In the song *Mastermind*, what type of drinks does Taylor refer to, which she compares herself to the liquor in?

7. In the song *The Alchemy*, what type of wine do the chemicals hit Taylor like?

10. In the song *champagne problems*, what brand of champagne did the subject of the song buy to celebrate an engagement?

14. In the song *You Need To Calm Down*, what brand of tequila are people taking shots at Taylor like at 7am?

MASTERMINDS

FOR EACH MASTER, ANSWER THESE
QUIZ QUESTIONS TO FIND CODE WORDS,
THEN GUESS WHAT THE CODE WORDS
HAVE IN COMMON

MASTER 7

1. The first name of one of Taylor's best friends and collaborators, who is also the lead vocalist of the band Bleachers.

2. Taylor's signature hand gesture, which she has said is a way of thanking crowds and telling them she loves them. She told the *Times* in 2011 that when a crowd is screaming really loudly she just wants to tell 'them I love them over and over, but sometimes the simplest thing to do is to make a sign with your hands.'

3. What type of jewel does Taylor bathe in in the *Look What You Made Me Do* music video?

4. What do the jokers dress up as in *Call It What You Want*?

MASTER 8

1. Taylor sings that she loved this city in *So Long,* _____.

2. In *long story short* Taylor sings about people who she's parted with missing her at the _____ _____ they used to hold the keys to.

3. In *All Too Well (10 Minute Version) (Taylor's Version)* what broke Taylor's skin and bones?

4. The creator and star of the comedy-drama television series *Fleabag,* who Taylor penned a heartfelt essay about for the *Times'* 100 Most Influential People of 2020 list.

FUN FACT: When Taylor missed Canada off the Eras Tour schedule, Prime Minister Justin Trudeau contacted her on X, writing: 'It's me, hi. I know places in Canada would love to have you. So, don't make it another cruel summer. We hope to see you soon.' Various other world leaders, such as the Chilean President and the mayor of Budapest, have also publicly reached out to Taylor asking her to bring the Eras Tour to their countries.

CONNECTIONS

IN EACH PUZZLE, FIND FOUR GROUPS OF FOUR WORDS, WHICH ARE CONNECTED BY A LINKING CATEGORY

Betty	Rose	Hayley	Dorothea
Lana	Florence	Sapphire	Phoebe
Ivy	Ruby	Emma	Daisy
Diamond	Wisteria	Amber	Clara

FOR THE SWIFTIES

Magic	Skirts	Lonely	Covert
Congressman	Sin	Bleachers	Heaven
Confused	Altruism	Free	Captain
T-Shirts	Madness	Narcissism	Happy

Delicate	You're On Your Own, Kid	Come Back... Be Here	Lover
my tears ricochet	Fearless	Mine	Mary's Song (Oh My My My)
I Knew You Were Trouble.	Love Story	Evermore	Shake It Off
Speak Now	willow	Is It Over Now?	All Too Well

FUN FACT CRYPTOGRAM

USE THE CODE BELOW TO REVEAL AN ENCRYPTED FUN FACT ABOUT TAYLOR

Some of the letters have been filled in for you. Work out the code by considering the placement of the letters you already know, revealing a hidden message. Use the key below to track which letters are linked to each number.

A	B	C	D	E	F	G	H	I	J	K	L	M
							4					
N	O	P	Q	R	S	T	U	V	W	X	Y	Z
	5					19		26		1		

— — — — — — '   — — Y — O — ' —   — O — H — — ,
22 15 16 18 11 22   9 22 1 3 5 18   20   23 5 9 4 11 18

H — — — O — — —   — — — — — — — — O — —   — O —
4 22 18 25 5 18 11 16   22 20 12 7 18 22 9 7 5 15 20   8 5 18

— — Y — O —   — O   — — — O — —   —
9 22 1 3 5 18   9 5   25 11 24 5 23 11   22

H O — — — — — — —   — — — — — ' — O   — — Y — O —
4 5 18 20 11 25 22 24 6   18 7 16 11 18   20 5   9 22 1 3 5 18

— O — —   — O — — — — — — — — — Y   U — — — —
18 5 16 11   24 5 23 12 11 9 7 9 7 2 11 3 1   19 15 9 7 3

— H —   W — —   — W — — — —   Y — — — —   O — — .
20 4 11   26 22 20   9 26 11 3 2 11   1 11 22 18 20   5 3 16

QUEENS AND KING OF KITTY TOWN

IT'S A TYPICAL TUESDAY NIGHT AND TAYLOR IS SITTING DOWN TO WRITE A SEISMIC SONG THAT WILL SOAR UP THE CHARTS, BREAK WORLD RECORDS, BOND FRIENDS, AND MEND BROKEN HEARTS

The song doesn't take her very long to complete, which is lucky because her beloved cats are demanding her attention. How many cuddles do each of her cats demand and what are their favorite pastimes other than being adored by Taylor?

1. Olivia likes reading Hollywood biographies.

2. Benjamin doesn't like Scrabble.

3. The cat who demanded the least cuddles also likes books.

4. The cat who likes sitting in plant pots demanded 12 cuddles.

Rules: Each item of the category is matched to one (and only one) other item in each different category. Once you have deduced one piece of information, you can tick that box and therefore rule out the other options in that category, placing a cross in those boxes. For example, if you know that one cat likes reading Hollywood biographies, you could tick the box that matches their name to that hobby and put a cross in the box that shows them having other hobbies, as you know they don't have those. Knowing this information will help you work out what the other cats might be doing and demanding. Using the clues and following the logic, complete the grid and find all the answers!

		Hobbies			Cuddles demanded		
		Sitting in plant pots	Reading Hollywood biographies	Playing Scrabble	4	7	12
Cats	Benjamin						
	Meredith						
	Olivia						
Cuddles demanded	4						
	7						
	12						

PICTURE PERFECT

....

SOLVE THESE PICTURE PUZZLES TO REVEAL SOME KILLER SONGS

....

1. C+ [donkey] + **&** + [dragon] **-GON**

2. DELHI [map of India] **-H** [cat] **+E**

3. [car] + [person digging] + [ant] **-T**

4.  −F+NO+ ¢

5.  +ERM+ −W

6.  +U+

7.  −D+ −ATRE

MASTERMINDS

FOR EACH MASTER, ANSWER THESE
QUIZ QUESTIONS TO FIND CODE WORDS,
THEN GUESS WHAT THE CODE WORDS
HAVE IN COMMON

MASTER 9

1. Which melancholic pop songstress's real name is Lizzie Grant?

2. Which indie folk rocker from California is one third of the supergroup boygenius?

3. Which Australian country singer married Nicole Kidman in 2006?

4. Which American indie folk band's name derives from the French for "good winter"?

MASTER 10

1. In which European city can you find the Rijksmuseum, Voldelpark and Anne Frank's House?

2. What kind of animal are Olivia Benson and Meredith Grey?

3. Which romantic occasion takes place on February 14th?

4. Which 2009 film starring Miley Cyrus features the Hoedown Throwdown?

FUN FACTS: Taylor's parents gave her a gender-neutral name so that if someone saw her name on a resumé when she was an adult she wouldn't be judged on the basis of her gender.

When Taylor was 10 years old she won a national poetry contest for a poem called 'There's a Monster in My Closet!'. When she was 14 she wrote a still-unpublished 300-page novel called 'A Girl Named Girl'. The plot is about a mother who wanted a son and instead had a girl. To this day, the draft is only in the possession of her parents, Andrea and Scott.

MEGAMASTER

....

WHAT DO THESE 5 SONGS HAVE IN COMMON?

....

1. *Mary's Song (Oh My My My)*

2. *Breathe*

3. *The Way I Loved You*

4. *Enchanted*

5 *I Wish You Would*

This one is tough, so there's a clue below ...

MEGAMASTER CLUE: There are at least thirteen items on the page opposite which are all mentioned in one of Taylor's songs. Find which items they are and connect them together to reveal a clue.

BEJEWELED

MATCH THE JEWEL OR PRECIOUS METAL TO WHAT TAYLOR USES IT TO DESCRIBE

amber

aquamarine

diamond

gold

moonstone

opal

pearl

rubies

sapphire

silver

cage *(So It Goes . . .)*

skies *(marjorie)*

swimming pool *(Slut!)*

Clutching *(But Daddy I Love Him)*

gave up *(Maroon)*

sky *(Untouchable)*

tears *(Bejeweled)*

aura *(Bejeweled)*

spoon *(I Bet You Think About Me)*

eyes *(ivy)*

SCREAMING COLOR

TAYLOR INCLUDES VIVID DESCRIPTIONS IN HER SONGS, OFTEN USING COLORS TO DESCRIBE FEELINGS, LOVERS, AND EVEN HERSELF

Can you find the colors in the wordsearch opposite?
For added amusement, see if you can remember
when she uses them!

amber	lilac
aurora borealis green	maroon
black	neon
blue	opal
bronze	orange
burgundy	purple-pink
cherry	red
crimson	rosy
flamingo pink	rust
golden	scarlet
greige	tangerine
grey	teal
indigo	ultraviolet
key lime green	white
lavender	

```
F O P A L A D Z M O V J T E Z X Y A S H Q O P U B
O A G O O D E N C R I M S O N K Z B F R R E U Z B
N Q V K W Q L G E A P S K G Q M N N C R S A V V L
P F G O L D E N R N Y U M T U J D V G S W P J V A
C H E R R Y Y Y F F G H R L D W D E M R Q Q J A C
R S X B N Z W D I B Y K R P O V B O M O E B W X K
O A E T L Z X H A K L C F V L U H U M V R I T J U
S M R M X U X S I O Q J N R A E L N Q P S A G K L
Y B H E I S E B D T C B L S Q N P K D I V K N E H
R E Y I Y D D C U O E F L I Q M U I Z H S E P G B
C R P W N P P O P R F H X A K G W E N M C Y D Y E
C W S A G D Q V O U G L H R V Z I R E K A L S L P
M C Y O H L I P E X Z U A Q W E N B B V R I H I L
Q T N E T H W G J H K Q N M P C N P U H L M Z L Q
W P M V M B S G O I A T R D I J P D T L E E M A B
Y X A L B Y P R U X U U A E Y N R F E J T G B C R
T H R Z N M T J Q A H K L N D R G U C R M R F I O
I P O E W Y E Y P A Q T U N G X P O S O O E O G N
Y T O L L J A B A Q M F C O V E N G P T S E B R Z
D N N Z E Q L T V T Z W B H P A R E N I S N I E E
K E E F J J T Z V A K J O T G O V I O O N E N Y N
K E F H X U X E G X J L Y T H C K Y N N U K E C E
Y J X A U R O R A B O R E A L I S G R E E N T R L
H G E D O K F U O A G H G A G K Q I V K Q U C C L
U L T R A V I O L E T O P T C D B D L T J G M M N
```

109

SUDOKLU

USE THE KEY TO FILL OUT THE MISSING
BOXES AND UNLOCK A SUDOKU PUZZLE

			4					
		9		I		3		4
4	A		B					C
6	7		G			C		
	D			4			6	
		H			E		3	5
A					4		8	F
E		1		F		H		
					G			

KEY

A = After Taylor Swift publicly endorsed two Democrats in Tennessee in an Instagram post in 2018, Donald Trump said he liked 'Taylor's music about 2_% less now'.

B = Due to a glitch in the Canadian version of iTunes, a Taylor Swift song titled '*Track 3*' that was just __ seconds of static noise was released in 2014. The track shot to the top of the iTunes Canada chart, prompting Taylor to joke that she's been, 'really overthinking this entire thing, I've been really trying too hard, clearly', on *Jimmy Kimmel Live!*.

C = The difference in age between Taylor and her brother, Austin, rounded to the nearest year.

D = Taylor won her first Video Music Award for best female video in 200_. Kanye West famously stormed the stage and took the microphone from Taylor to say that, 'Beyoncé had one of the best videos of all time'.

E = Joe Jonas reportedly broke up with Taylor on a 2_ second phone call, which is also the length of the intro to the song *Last Kiss*, which many believe is about Joe Jonas.

F = Number of letters in the second name of Joe Alwyn's pseudonym when he collaborated on songs with Taylor.

G = The number of letters in the original name of the second album Taylor re-recorded.

H = How many blue eyes are referenced in *State of Grace*?

I = Harvey Weinstein asked Taylor to write a song for the romantic comedy _____ *Chance*. The song, called *Sweeter Than Fiction*, earned Taylor her second Golden Globe nomination.

SLOPING CURSIVE LETTERS

Write the answer to each question in the corresponding row or column on the crossword below.

ACROSS

2. What is the name of the main character in the Lewis Carroll book alluded to in the *1989* track *Wonderland*, which references falling down a rabbit hole and the Cheshire Cat's smile?

4. Which track on *Fearless* borrows themes from Shakespeare's *Romeo and Juliet*?

5. In *the tortured poets department*, alongside Patti Smith, which famous poet who stayed at the Chelsea Hotel and whose works include the poem *Do Not Go Gentle into that Good night* and the play *Under Milk Wood*, does Taylor reference? (Fun facts: this poet used to drink regularly at the nearby White Horse Tavern, where he allegedly drank himself to death. Taylor's song *White Horse*, from the *Fearless* album, has been compared to the song *the tortured poets department* in the sections where Taylor gives a reality check to the subject of her song, telling them they're living in the real world rather than a fairytale or famous literary era.)

6. Which track on *the tortured poets department* album alludes to *The Rime of the Ancient Mariner*, which is about a sailor who kills a large seabird, after which bad things start happening, and his fellow seamen make him wear the dead bird around his neck?

7. In *Reputation*'s *This is Why We Can't Have Nice Things*, which F. Scott Fitzgerald novel does Taylor draw from, about a character who is famous for throwing lavish parties?

11. Which track on *the tortured poets department* album references the ancient Greek philosopher Aristotle?

13. Which novel by Nathaniel Hawthorne, set in Massachusetts during the years 1642 to 1649 about a woman named Hester Prynne who must wear a red 'A' (for adultery) after she conceives a child out of wedlock, is referenced in *Love Story* and *New Romantics*?

14. Which bonus track of the *folklore* album refers to England's Lake District, which during the 18th and 19th centuries was home to a group of esteemed writers known as The Lake Poets? These poets include William Wordsworth, who Taylor may be paying homage to when she references a sleaze asking her what are her 'words worth?' in the song.

15. Which character of a boy who never grows up is referenced on both *folklore* and *the tortured poets department*?

DOWN

1. In *Lover*'s *The Archer*, which classic nursery rhyme is quoted, with reference to the king's horses and the king's men?

3. Which track on *evermore* features a reference to King Midas, who could turn anything to gold by touching it? In the song, about turning down a marriage proposal, she refers to this type of magical touch on the door of a Chevy.

8. In *The Prophecy* on *the tortured poets department*, who does Taylor reference getting bitten, in a nod to the story of The Garden of Eden?

9. Which track on *Red* references the Shakespeare play, *All's Well That Ends Well*?

10. In Robert Frost's poem, *The Road Not Taken*, he writes: 'Two roads diverged in a wood, and I– / I took the one less traveled by, And that has made all the difference.' Taylor has lines similar to this on *The Outside*, from her 2006 debut album, as well as which song (about secret affairs) on *folklore*?

12. The opening line of *Reputation*'s *Getaway Car* is a play on the famous opening line: 'It was the best of times, the worst of times', of which Charles Dickens novel?

FOR THE SWIFTIES

BAD BLOOD

BACK IN THE BAD BLOOD BATTLE OF 2015, CATASTROPHE SECURED A DECISIVE VICTORY OVER HER NEMESIS, ARSYN, WITH SUPPORT FROM HER SUPER SQUAD

But since then, tables have been turning and bridges have been burning, and Arsyn has stolen some of the squad to her troop, the Band of Bombshells, away from Captain Catastrophe's Super Squad. A new battle is brewing – which weapons will Catastrophe's team, the Super Squad, use to take down their nemeses in the Band of Bombshells?

1. The four Super Squad members are: Mother Chucker; the one fighting Headmistress; the one with a gun; and Arsyn's vanquisher.

2. Slay Z's nemesis is neither Arsyn nor Knockout.

3. Arsyn is vanquished by a lipstick.

4. The axe's wielder comes later in the alphabet than she who wields the icicle.

5. Of Frostbyte and Mother Chucker, one bears an icicle while the other fights Knockout.

6. Headmistress is not the one attacked by the axe.

		Weapon used				Band of Bombshells member			
		Lipstick	Gun	Axe	Icicle	Arsyn	Headmistress	Cut Throat	Knockout
Super Squad member	Catastrophe								
	Frostbyte								
	Mother Chucker								
	Slay-Z								
Band of Bombshells member	Arsyn								
	Headmistress								
	Cut Throat								
	Knockout								

Rules: Each item of the category is matched to one (and only one) other item in each different category. Once you have deduced one piece of information, you can tick that box and therefore rule out the other options in that category, placing a cross in those boxes. For example, if you know that Mother Chucker and the Super Squad member fighting Headmistress are different characters, you can put a cross in the box showing Mother Chucker fighting Headmistress. And once you know, for example, that Arsyn is vanquished by a lipstick, you can put a tick in the box showing her getting vanquished by a lipstick and crosses in the boxes showing her getting vanquished by other weapons as well as in the boxes showing other Band of Bombshell members getting vanquished by the lipstick. Knowing this information will help you work out what other characters are up to. You may need to look at clues considering the grid both horizontally and vertically, as some clues will give you answers to different sections of the grid. Using the clues and following the logic, complete the grid and find all the answers!

SNAKES AND STONES

CONNECT THE SNAKE'S HEAD AND TAIL TO COMPLETE ITS BODY

The numbers around the outside of the grid tell you how many pieces of snake are to be placed in each row and column. Within each square the snake can either move in a straight line or turn at a 90-degree angle.

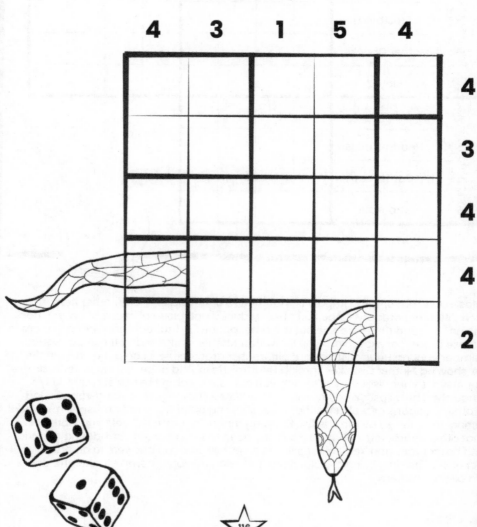

SPELLING VAULT

SPELLING IS FUN!

Join Taylor in her love of words and find as many as you can using the central letter. Each word must have a minimum of four letters and letters can be used more than once. For bonus points, find the Taylor Swift related word from the vault which uses all the letters!

4-letter words:

5-letter words:

6-letter words:

7-letter words:

8-letter word:

LABYRINTH

HELP TAYLOR FIND THE LOVE AT
THE CENTER OF THE LABYRINTH
OF HER MIND

SINGONYMS

WHICH TAYLOR SWIFT SONG TITLES ARE HIDDEN IN THESE SYNONYMS?

1. Wrong Deity

2. It's Pleasant Having A Buddy

3. The Final Fantastic USA Lineage

4. Transparent Rope

5. Bubbly Issues

6. No Corpse, No Felony

7. Purple Mist

8. Avenger Poop

9. Sugary Zilch

10. Newly Out Of Prison

11. It's the Darned Time of Year

12. The Mistreated Rhymester Unit

13. However, Father, I am Smitten With This Male

STAY IN STYLE

TAYLOR IS A MASTER OF REINVENTION AND HAS RADICALLY DIFFERENT STYLES ACROSS ERAS

She also sings about clothes in her songs for added texture and detail. Can you spot all the items hiding in the wordsearch opposite?

bag

ball gown

baseball cap

big coat

blouse

buttons on a coat

cardigan

cloaks

crown

faded blue jeans

glasses

gloves

high heels

lilac short skirt

little black dress

locket

mittens

necklace

necktie

organic shoes

party dress

plaid shirt

ring

scarf

sneakers

suit and tie

sweater

sweatshirt

vintage dresses

white t-shirt

white veil

wine-stained dress

your jacket

```
Q O W D M E O I V I N T A G E D R E S S E S V F O
S Z V R I N G P G S Q W Y B P C G Q B I V J B A T
A U B E E Q F Z L N H I T M F Y K L Z R O O T D B
I N I O C B O H S A E A V Q W J S M O L K D R E U
V H P U J C R O L K I C I D Y O H B Y V T Z I D T
B K O F L C G I P U R D K J M V F U S L E O N B T
X Z B U E B A Y K P L G S L P D I K W I Z S V L O
T Z E W E U N A P Z I W G H A K O H E T C W Y U N
Z V G H T L I W A O L S R N I C F O A T W E Q E S
N E Q I R O C G R W A O N R W R E R T L I A K J O
E I B T V C S Q T H C L Y J I A T J S E N T A E N
H Q L E L K H U Y I S Y M L N N C B H B S E Z A A
I K O T M E O N D T H O D S E T A A I L N R C N C
G X U S T T E E R E O U Y U S N R S R A E Y R S O
H C S H E E S C E V R R B I T L D E T C A O O P A
H L E I D N Y K S E T J I T A J I B H K K D W V T
E O X R X Y L T S I S A G A I F G A S D E E N H T
E A V T I D C I S L K C C N N Y A L Q R R K T I N
L K W E G G G E A V I K O D E K N L H E S E J V O
S S S W G L K G H K R E A T D M R C L S Z B O U O
F G C H F P A J A P T T T I D Z U A Y S Q N A X N
R D A A P C X S R Y M C K E R D Y P I Z H O I G C
X M R T P J M R S D P G J O E B A L L G O W N G I
I E F O I W D N L E B M V Y S B F X U N F G P E R
E Q E N F K L T G X S V B A S F C M I T T E N S J
```

FUN FACT: When major clothing company Abercrombie and Fitch released a t-shirt emblazoned with the phrase "More Boyfriends Than T.S." in 2013, her fans banded together in protest against the company and its products via social media. The company later apologized and pulled the merchandise from all its stores.

THROUGH THE ERAS

CAN YOU PUT THESE KEY MOMENTS IN TAYLOR'S LIFE IN DATE ORDER?

Some key dates are already filled in for reference.

A. Grammy Awards where Taylor is nominated for her first Grammy, in this instance, for Best New Artist

B. First date of the *Eras Tour*

C. Taylor wins Album of The Year at the Grammys for *Midnights*, making her the first artist to win that award four times

D. Release of first album, *Taylor Swift*

E. *Forbes* declares Taylor a billionaire

F. Taylor wipes clean all her social media accounts

G. Release of her first single, *Tim McGraw*

H. *Shake It Off* becomes Taylor's first song to debut at number 1 in the US charts

I. Taylor wins best Music Video at VMAs and Kanye storms the stage

J. *the tortured poets department* album released

K. Record broken for the fastest selling digital single in history with *We Are Never Ever Getting Back Together*

L. Taylor releases her first re-recorded album: *Fearless (Taylor's Version)*

M. Taylor named *TIME*'s Person of the Year, the first to be recognized for 'achievement in the arts'

N. Taylor wins her first Grammy

Date	Event
13 December 1989	Taylor Swift is born
19 June 2006	
24 October 2006	
10 February 2008	
11 November 2008	Second album *Fearless* released
13 September 2009	
7 November 2009	Host and musical guest on Saturday Night Live
31 January 2010	
14 August 2012	
6 September 2014	
27 October 2014	Album *1989* is released
18 August 2017	
23 August 2019	Her seventh album *Lover* is released
9 April 2021	
17 March 2023	
13 October 2023	*The Eras Tour* opens in cinemas
6 December 2023	
4 February 2024	
2 April 2024	
19 April 2024	

CRYPTIC CROSSWORD

A PUZZLE FOR LOVERS OF WILY WORDPLAY!

ACROSS

3. Frozen chilli [3, 5]
6. Abnormal nail span envy prompts birth state [12]
7. Unconventional lead role: man of courage is coming after antique without hearing he must wait in line [4-4]
8. This pea knows how to keep it together [5, 3]
9. Knave and social insect oscillating is collaborator [4, 8]
10. High profile prize in some measure an Instagram myth [6]

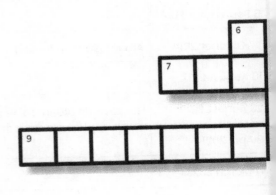

DOWN

1. Cutting off limbs again, but not in the morning, gives esteem and album title [10]
2. Underground storage room for gymnastics equipment? [3, 6]
4. Like a polaroid picture? Putrid. 1989/6 [5, 2, 3]
5. The boy goat starts, the lion is hidden, finished by broadcasting with energy for member of the top 0.1% [11]

FOR THE SWIFTIES

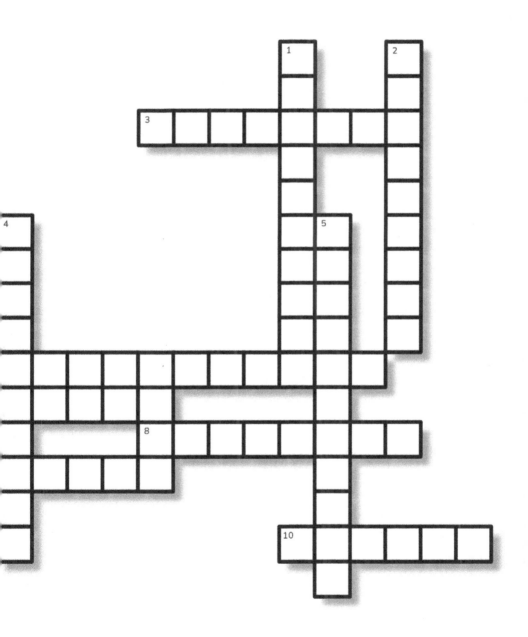

TAYLOR AND ME AND YOU

FILL IN THE BLANK SPACES TO COMPARE YOUR AND YOUR BESTIE'S SWIFTIE FAVORITES

My favorite Taylor Swift album

Your favorite Taylor Swift album

My favorite Taylor Swift song

Your favorite Taylor Swift song

My favorite Taylor Swift lyric

Your favorite Taylor Swift lyric

My favorite Taylor Swift outfit

Your favorite Taylor Swift outfit

My favorite Taylor Swift music video

Your favorite Taylor Swift music video

If I was Taylor for the day I would ...

If you were Taylor for the day you would ...

STUMBLING HOLOGRAMS

AFTER HER EX RUSTED HER SPARKLING SUMMER, TAYLOR WAS HAUNTED BY HOLOGRAMS OF HIM STUMBLING INTO HER APARTMENT

Each time he is entwined with a new flame he's just been on a date with. All the while, Taylor's been on his mind too. Where did Taylor's ex go with each date and how many memories of Taylor resurfaced on each date?

1. Taylor imagined her ex on dates with the following four different people on four different dates: hanging out with a girl called Sophia; taking someone else to a concert; running around Brooklyn with a different girl; and perusing records with some boy called Marcus.

2. The date in Brooklyn brought 13 different memories of Taylor to her ex's mind.

3. Taylor's ex's date with Chloe surfaced more memories of Taylor than the date with Sophia did, but not as many as the date with Sam did.

4. The date at the chicken shop brought Taylor to her ex's mind 5 times.

5. Chloe ordered a drink at a bar that she can't get in the UK on her date with Taylor's ex.

6. The date in Brixton brought the most memories of Taylor to her ex's mind.

7. Neither Sam nor Sophia have ever been to LA.

		Date location				Venue				Memories surfaced			
		Brixton, London	Soho, London	Brooklyn, New York	Hollywood, Los Angeles	A chicken shop	A bar	A concert venue	A vinyl record shop	5	8	13	75
Character	Chloe												
	Sam												
	Sophia												
	Marcus												
Venue	A chicken shop												
	A bar												
	A concert venue												
	A vinyl record shop												
Memories surfaced	5												
	8												
	13												
	75												

Rules: Each item of the category is matched to one (and only one) other item in each different category. Once you have deduced one piece of information, you can tick that box and therefore rule out the other options in that category, placing a cross in those boxes. For example, if you know that Sophia and the person who Taylor's ex took to a concert are different people, you can put a cross in the box showing Taylor's ex taking Sophia to a concert. And once you know that the date that went to the chicken shop brought Taylor to her ex's mind 5 times, you can put a tick in the box connecting the chicken shop and 5 memories and crosses in the boxes for 5 memories being linked to other venues as well as for the chicken shop being linked to other numbers of memories. Knowing this information will help you work out what other characters are up to. You may need to look at clues considering the grid both horizontally and vertically, as some clues will give you answers to different sections of the grid. Using the clues and following the logic, complete the grid and find all the answers!

129

ENDGAME

CRACK THE FINAL CODE

You are a _____(1) _____(2)

and _____(3)

will _____(4)

you to the ____(5)____(6)___ ____(7)___(8)___(9)

1. The secret code from Music in My Mind on page 49.

2. Where are the secret gardens Taylor escapes to?
   In her _____.

3. Buried even deeper than Taylor's hatchet on page 47, this hidden word hides in the row below and was not one of your wordsearch clues.

4. In the cryptogram on pages 58–59, what does 15, 16, 20, 17 spell?

5. What is the letter that comes before c in the 13th answer of the Sloping Cursive Letters crossword on pages 112–113?

6. Which letter appears the most frequently in the 13th answer to the singonym on page 72?

7. In the crossword Get In, Let's Drive on pages 20–21, what are the two middle letters of the second word of the answer to question 13? This is also the 13th letter of the alphabet.

8. Blue, brown, bright, beautiful, wide, wild, tired, twinkling, hollow, half-moon, green, indigo and opal. These are 13 examples of how Taylor describes what? If spelled how it sounds with one letter, what letter would this be?

9. What is the last letter in the last word of the last answer of the Eras Tour Quiz on pages 68–69?

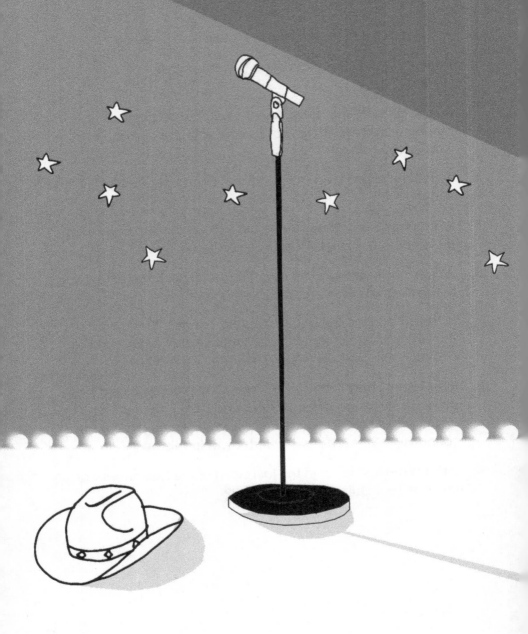

ANSWERS

p.10 SINGONYMS

1. *Wildest Dreams*
2. *Hits Different*
3. *Getaway Car*
4. *Suburban Legends*
5. *The Smallest Man Who Ever Lived*
6. *Stay Beautiful*
7. *A Perfectly Good Heart*
8. *Fortnight*
9. *Love Story*
10. *White Horse*
11. *Tell Me Why*
12. *Jump Then Fall*
13. *Come In With The Rain*

p.11 SPELLING VAULT

8-letters: epiphany

7-letters: hyenine, paphian

6-letters: hyphae, hyaena, hyphen, happen, hippie, peahen, heinie, hinnie

5-letters: heapy, happy, hippy, hypha, hinny, hayey, hyena, ephah, happi, henna

4-letters: hype, hiya, nyah, yeah, ayah, epha, heap, haen, haha

p.12 'TIS THE DAMN SEASON

Summer (Total 13): *august, Better Than Revenge, betty, Hits Different, Love Story, Lover, peace, seven, Starlight, Suburban Legends, The Smallest Man Who Ever Lived, Tim McGraw, You're On Your Own Kid*

Fall/Autumn (Total 5): *All Too Well, Cornelia Street, marjorie, Red, The Best Day*

Winter (Total 3): *Christmas Tree Farm, evermore, Paper Rings*

Spring (Total 2): *I Bet You Think About Me, ivy*

p.14 POP QUIZ

1. b. *1989*
2. c. 13
3. a. Sagittarius
4. c. Alison
5. a. Andrea
6. c. Austin
7. b. Taffy
8. b. Scott
9. b. *marjorie*
10. a. opera singing
11. b. vodka diet coke
12. a. Cheeseburger, fries, and a chocolate shake
13. c. millipede
14. c. Friends
15. a. a stockbroker
16. b. *Our Song*
17. b. Taylor Swift
18. a. 39,000
19. b. 592,000
20. c. Justin Timberlake
21. b. 2009
22. a. 2011
23. c. It was scheduled for 13 hours and took 15
24. a. An Easter egg hunt
25. b. Liz Rose
26. a. Wonderstruck
27. c. Max Martin
28. b. *We Are Never Ever Getting Back Together*
29. b. 10 minutes
30. a. Sadie Sink
31. c. Imaginative, smart, hard working
32. b. *Wildest Dreams*
33. c. *You Are in Love*
34. a. *I Wish You Would*
35. c. She had been called for jury duty in Nashville the next morning (which she attended).
36. b. Calvin Harris
37. a. Nils Sjöberg
38. c. That karma is real
39. b. Six minutes
40. a. *Delicate*
41. a. Loie Fuller
42. b. The Beatles
43. c. *It's Nice To Have a Friend*
44. a. Idris Elba
45. c. Jack Antonoff
46. b. Tyler Swift
47. a. *Miss Americana*
48. b. *Soon You'll Get Better*
49. c. *Clean*
50. c. Healing people
51. a. Augustine, James and Betty
52. b. Joe Alwyn
53. c. Lavender Haze
54. c. *Question…?*
55. c. *Labyrinth*
56. a. *Amsterdam*
57. c. Harvard
58. b. Roberto Cavalli
59. b. 13
60. b. 300 million

p.19 SNAKES AND STONES

p.20 LET'S DRIVE

ACROSS

4. *Out Of The Woods*
6. *Our Song*
7. *Kings of My Heart*
8. *Wonderland*
9. *Picture To Burn*
10. *So High School*
11. *Tim McGraw*
12. *Invisible string*
13. *Cruel Summer*
15. *All Too Well*
16. *The Bolter*

DOWN

1. *The Best Day*
2. *Getaway Car*
3. *You Belong with Me*
5. *Cornelia Street*
14. *Red*

p.22 FUN FACT CRYPTOGRAM

Taylor has a framed photo of the moment Kanye West hijacked her acceptance speech during the 2009 VMAs in her living room in Nashville hanging above a handwritten note that reads: Life is full of little interruptions.

A	B	C	D	E	F	G	H	I	J	K	L	M
4	12	1	2	21	9	20	15	13	6	10	18	5

N	O	P	Q	R	S	T	U	V	W	X	Y	Z
3	8	14	16	24	23	26	22	7	11	17	25	19

p.24 ONCE UPON A TIME

Better Man: 4am
Electric Touch: 8:05
I Bet You Think About Me: 3am
I Wish You Would: 2am
Mine: 2:30
Last Kiss: 1:58
Lavender Haze: 12:00

p.26 BIG, OLD CITIES

p.28 CONNECT THE DOTS

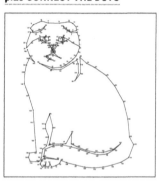

p.29 MISS AMERICANA

1. Florida
2. Georgia
3. Los Angeles
4. Las Vegas
5. New York
6. Pennsylvania
7. Rhode Island
8. St. Louis
9. Tennessee
10. Texas
11. Tupelo

p.30 SUDOKLU

a) 4
b) 7
c) 3
d) 2
e) 5
f) 8
g) 9
h) 1
i) 6

4	1	6	2	8	3	5	9	7
3	7	2	5	4	9	8	6	1
5	8	9	7	6	1	4	2	3
8	3	4	9	1	2	7	5	6
9	5	1	8	7	6	2	3	4
2	6	7	3	5	4	9	1	8
7	9	8	1	3	5	6	4	2
6	2	3	4	9	7	1	8	5
1	4	5	6	2	8	3	7	9

p.32 ALIBIS

Athena was in the fishing boat and drank 2 glasses of wine.

Este's husband was in the wine bar and drank 4 glasses of wine.

Este was at Olive Garden and drank 3 glasses of wine.

		Location			# glasses of wine		
		Olive garden	Wine bar	Fishing boat	2	3	4
Character	Athena			x	x		
	Este's husband		x				x
	Este	x				x	
# glasses of wine	2			x			
	3	x					
	4		x				

p.34 EMOJI MOJO

p.36 FUN FACT CRYPTOGRAM

Taylor featured Blake Lively and Ryan Reynolds' baby daughter James Reynolds saying the word "gorgeous" for the first line of the song *Gorgeous* on the album *reputation*.

A	B	C	D	E	F	G	H	I	J	K	L	M
13	2	5	22	17	18	19	20	26	21	15	25	23
N	O	P	Q	R	S	T	U	V	W	X	Y	Z
8	7	14	3	6	4	24	11	16	9	1	12	10

p.38 OUT OF THE WOODS

p.39 SPELLING VAULT

8-letters: folklore

6-letters: looker, relook, keeler

5-letters: kloof

4-letters: flok, fork, kerf, koel, kolo, kore, look, rook, folk, keel, kook, leek, reek

p.40 QUICK TRIVIA QUIZ

1. James Taylor
2. *The Star-Spangled Banner*
3. Scott Borchetta
4. no its becky
5. J
6. *Les Misérables*
7. Not a lot going on at the moment
8. woodvale

p.42 WILD JOY

ACROSS

4. Vulture
5. Cat
7. Horse
9. Wolf
10. Golden Retriever
12. Firefly
14. Moth
15. Dog
16. Snake

DOWN

1. Flamingo
2. Crickets
3. Butterfly
6. Phoenix
8. Bear
11. Dragon
13. Lion

p.44 FOR A MONTH

Lover	January
Fortnight	February
High Infidelity	April
You All Over Me	June
Last Kiss	July
Tim McGraw	September
Innocent	September
Call It What You Want	November
champagne problems	November
Out Of The Woods	December

p.46 WHEN THE CLAWS COME OUT

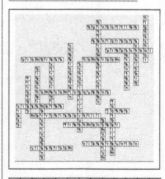

Hidden word = Karma

p.48 A SICK BEAT

Shake It Off (160bpm)

the last great american dynasty (148bpm)

cardigan (130bpm)

Karma (90bpm)

willow (81bpm)

p.49 MUSIC IN MY MIND

M (medley)

A

S (saxophone)

T (time)

E (electric guitar)

R (refrain)

p.50 TEACH SOME LESSONS

1	2	3	4	5	6	7	8	9	10	11	12	13
l	z	u	x	c	r	n	p	q	d	o	h	j

14	15	16	17	18	19	20	21	22	23	24	25	26
t	a	v	w	b	y	f	i	m	k	s	g	e

bittersweet sixteen
bleachers
cheer captain
class reunion
classmates
classroom
college
crazy
extra credit
first day
football team
freshman year
gymnasium
high school
homecoming queens
homeroom
jokes
marching band
marry kiss or kill
prep school
prom dress
schoolgirl crush
schoolyard
senior boys
seventeen
spin bottles

p.52 SUDOKLU

A) 7
B) 5
C) 6
D) 1
E) 8
F) 4
G) 2
H) 9
I) 3

9	6	7	1	2	3	8	4	5
4	8	3	6	7	5	9	1	2
5	2	1	9	4	8	7	3	6
2	3	8	7	5	1	4	6	9
7	9	5	8	6	4	1	2	3
1	4	6	2	3	9	5	8	7
3	5	2	4	1	7	6	9	8
6	1	9	5	8	2	3	7	4
8	7	4	3	9	6	2	5	1

p.56 LOVE TRIANGLE

James was wearing Levi's and danced with 1 person.

Augustine was wearing sweatshirt and danced with 2 people.

Betty was wearing a cardigan and danced with 3 people.

		Clothing		# dances		
		Cardigan	Levi's	Sweatshirt	3	2	1
Character	James		x				x
	Augustine			x		x	
	Betty	x			x		
# dances	3	x					
	2			x			
	1		x				

p.58 FUN FACT CRYPTOGRAM

In 2010 at 20 years old, Taylor won a Grammy for album of the year for Fearless, making her the youngest person to receive the award.

A	B	C	D	E	F	G	H	I	J	K	L	M
16	3	21	2	17	1	25	5	4	8	20	22	7

N	O	P	Q	R	S	T	U	V	W	X	Y	Z
18	6	13	12	10	24	15	26	23	11	14	19	9

p.60 LOOK WHAT YOU MADE ME DUET

Bad Blood (Remix)	Kendrick Lamar
Both of Us	B.o.B
Breathe	Colbie Caillat
Castles Crumbling	Hayley Williams
coney island	The National
Electric Touch	Fall Out Boy
Everything Has Changed	Ed Sheeran
exile	Bon Iver
Florida!!!	Florence + the Machine
Fortnight	Post Malone
I Bet You Think About Me	Chris Stapleton
Don't Wanna Live Forever	ZAYN
Karma (Remix)	Ice Spice

Lover (Remix)	Shawn Mendes
ME!	Brendon Urie
no body, no crime	HAIM
Nothing New	Phoebe Bridgers
Safe & Sound	The Civil Wars
Snow On The Beach	Lana Del Rey
Soon You'll Get Better	The Chicks
That's When	Keith Urban
The Last Time	Gary Lightbody
You All Over Me	Maren Morris

p.64 LOVE STORIES

p.64 FLASHING LIGHTS

p.66 COME IN WITH THE RAIN

ACROSS
3. Hey Stephen
6. Tied Together With A Smile
7. The Albatross
9. Dear John
10. peace
12. Midnight Rain
14. Cold As You
15. The Black Dog
16. Last Kiss
17. London Boy
18. Sparks Fly

DOWN
1. happiness
2. Everything Has Changed
4. Stay Beautiful
5. ME!
6. The Way I Loved You
8. How You Get The Girl
11. Clean
13. Forever And Always

p.68 THE ERAS TOUR QUIZ

1. c. 2.3
2. b. Mandy Moore
3. b. A stadium show every single night for the next 2.5 years
4. c. $1 billion
5. b. $100,000
6. a. 69,000
7. a. Brazil
8. b. 2 hours 48 minutes
9. a. Los Angeles
10. b. 22
11. c. 50 meters and 350 hours
12. b. 2,100
13. c. A janitor cart

p.70 SNAKES AND STONES

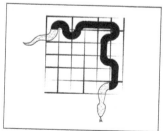

p.71 SPELLING VAULT

8-letters: t-swizzle, swizzles, zestiest, zestless

7-letters: twizzle, sizeist, tzitzit, tweezes

6-letters: tizzes, zizzes, tzetze

5-letters: zests, zills, zitis, zizit

4-letters: zits, zill, tizz, zizz

p.72 SINGONYMS

1. *Bye Bye Baby*
2. *Speak Now*
3. *Last Kiss*
4. *Holy Ground*
5. *Sad Beautiful Tragic*
6. *Begin Again*
7. *The Moment I Knew*
8. *Girl At Home*
9. *Blank Space*
10. *Call It What You Want*
11. *I Forgot That You Existed*
12. *London Boy*
13. *Untouchable*

p.73 MASTERMINDS

MASTER 1:
1. Apple (as in, the Big Apple)
2. Welcome (as in, Welcome to New York, a Taylor Swift song)
3. Liberty (as in, the Statue of Liberty)
4. Times (as in, Times Square)
5. Coney Island (as in, part of Brooklyn, New York)

Answer: New York

MASTER 2:
1. Stephen (as in, Cat Stevens)
2. Tom (as in, tomcat)
3. Andrew Lloyd Webber (as in, writer of the music for Cats, the musical, which Taylor starred in the film version of)
4. Benjamin (as in, the name of one of Taylor's cats)
5. Olivia Benson (as in, the name of one of Taylor's cats)

Answer: Cat

MASTER 3:
1. Dress (as in, wedding dress)
2. Ring (as in, wedding ring)
3. Cake (as in, wedding cake)
4. Speech (as in, wedding speech)

Answer: weddings

MASTER 4:
1. Maroon
2. Blood
3. Burgundy
4. Cherry

Answer: shades of red

MASTER 5:
1. Rainbow
2. Fair
3. Haze
4. Sun

Answer: weather

MASTER 6:
1. Time
2. Wine
3. Spirit
4. Trust

Answer: *Death By A Thousand Cuts*

p.76 A ROYAL COMPETITION

Lady Danielle desires the ring and her shoe size is 5.

Lady Este desires the title and her shoe size is 8.

Lady Alana desires The D*** and her shoe size is 3.

		Desires			Shoe size		
		The ring	The title	The D***	3	5	8
Character	Lady Danielle	x				x	
	Lady Este		x				x
	Lady Alana			x	x		
Shoe size	3			x			
	5	x					
	8		x				

p.78 DESCRAMBLE

1. *Epiphany*
2. *The Albatross*
3. *The Prophecy*
4. *Gorgeous*
5. *mirrorball*
6. *Wonderland*
7. *White Horse*
8. *Superman*
9. *willow*
10. *New Year's Day*

p.80 THROUGH THE GARDEN GATE

p.82 FUN FACT CRYPTOGRAM

When Taylor was twelve years old, computer repairman and local musician Ronnie Cremer taught her to play guitar. The first song she learned to play was Sixpence None the Richer's hit *Kiss Me*.

A	B	C	D	E	F	G	H	I	J	K	L	M
17	19	6	16	4	25	9	10	8	5	22	14	13

N	O	P	Q	R	S	T	U	V	W	X	Y	Z
2	7	15	18	20	1	24	26	23	12	21	3	11

p.84 CONNECT THE DOTS

p.85 GETAWAY CAR

p.86 IF THIS WAS A MOVIE

Crazier	Hannah Montana: The Movie (2009)
Today Was a Fairytale	Valentine's Day (2010)
Safe & Sound	The Hunger Games (2012)
Sweeter Than Fiction	One Chance (2013)
Don't Wanna Live Forever	Fifty Shades Darker (2017)
Beautiful Ghosts	Cats (2019)
Only the Young	Miss Americana (2020)
Carolina	Where the Crawdads Sing (2022)

p.88 SUDOKLU

9
2
8
4
1
6
3
5
7

6	5	7	9	8	4	3	1	2
1	3	8	7	2	5	6	9	4
4	2	9	3	1	6	7	8	5
9	1	6	8	4	2	5	7	3
5	7	4	1	6	3	8	2	9
3	8	2	5	7	9	4	6	1
2	9	5	6	3	8	1	4	7
8	4	1	2	5	7	9	3	6
7	6	3	4	9	1	2	5	8

p.90 DRINKS IN THE BAR

ACROSS

2. Whiskey
5. Rosé
6. Champagne
8. Liquor
9. Bottle
11. Screw-top
12. Wine
13. Beer
15. Old Fashioned
16. Stained

DOWN

1. Merlot
3. Island Breeze
4. Cocktails
7. White
10. Dom Pérignon
14. Patrón

p.92 MASTERMINDS

MASTER 7:
1. Jack
2. Heart
3. Diamonds
4. Kings
Answer: playing cards

MASTER 8:
1. London (as in London Bridge)
2. Golden Gates (as in the Golden Gate Bridge)
3. Brooklyn (as in Brooklyn Bridge)
4. Phoebe Waller-Bridge
Answer: bridges

p.94 CONNECTIONS

CONNECTION 1

Names in song titles: Betty; Clara; Dorothea; Emma

Featured artists: Hayley (Williams, *Castles Crumbling*); Florence (+ the Machine, *Florida!!!*); Phoebe (Bridgers, *Nothing New*); Lana (Del Rey, *Snow On The Beach*)

Gemstones featured in lyrics: Sapphire (*Bejeweled*); Ruby (*Maroon*); Diamond (various); Amber (*marjorie*)

Flowers/plants featured in lyrics: Rose (various); ivy (*ivy*); Daisy (*Don't Blame Me*); Wisteria (*the lakes*)

CONNECTION 2

Blank Space: magic; madness; heaven; sin

22: happy; free; confused; lonely

Anti-Hero: covert; narcissism; altruism; congressman

You Belong With Me: skirts; t-shirts; captain; bleachers

CONNECTION 3

Punctuation: Come Back...Be Here; I Knew You Were Trouble.; Is It Over Now?; Mary's Song (Oh My, My, My)

Track fives: All Too Well (Red), Delicate (reputation); my tears ricochet (folklore); You're On Your Own Kid (Midnights)

Album title tracks: evermore; Fearless; Lover; Speak Now

Lead singles: ME! (Lover); Mine (Speak Now); Shake It Off (1989); willow (evermore)

p.96 FUN FACT CRYPTOGRAM

Andrea, Taylor's mother, harbored aspirations for Taylor to become a horseback rider, so Taylor rode competitively until she was twelve years old.

A	B	C	D	E	F	G	H	I	J	K	L	M
22	25	24	16	11	8	17	4	7	14	6	3	23

N	O	P	Q	R	S	T	U	V	W	X	Y	Z
15	5	12	13	18	20	9	19	2	26	21	1	10

p.98 QUEEN AND KING OF KITTY TOWN

Benjamin's hobby is sitting in pot plants and he demands 12 cuddles.

Meredith's hobby is playing Scrabble and she demands 7 cuddles.

Olivia's hobby is reading Hollywood biographies and she demands 4 cuddles.

		Hobbies			Cuddles demanded		
		Sitting in plant pots	Reading hollywood biographies	Playing Scrabble	4	7	12
Cats	Benjamin	X					X
	Meredith			X	X		
	Olivia		X	X			
Cuddles demanded	4		X				
	7			X			
	12	X					

p.100 PICTURE PERFECT

1. Cassandra
2. Delicate
3. cardigan
4. Innocent
5. Mastermind
6. Manuscript
7. Breathe

p.102 MASTERMINDS

MASTER 9:
1. Lana Del Ray
2. Phoebe Bridgers
3. Keith Urban
4. Bon Iver

Answer: collaborators

MASTER 10:
1. Amsterdam
2. Cats
3. Valentine's Day
4. *Hannah Montana The Movie*

Answer: movies Taylor has been in

p.104 MEGAMASTER

They all feature a reference to 2am.

These all feature in *All Too Well (10 Minute Version) (Taylor's Version)*.

p.106 BEJEWELED

amber	skies (*marjorie*)
aquamarine	swimming pool (*Slut!*)
diamond	sky (*Untouchable*)
gold	cage (*So It Goes...*)
moonstone	aura (*Bejeweled*)
opal	eyes (*ivy*)
pearl	clutched (*But Daddy I Love Him*)
rubies	given up (*Maroon*)
sapphire	tears (*Bejeweled*)
silver	spoon (*I Bet You Think About Me*)

p.108 SCREAMING COLOR

[word search grid]

p.110 SUDOKLU

A) 5
B) 8
C) 2
D) 9
E) 7
F) 6
G) 3
H) 4
I) 1

1	6	3	4	2	5	9	7	8
8	2	9	7	1	6	3	5	4
4	5	7	8	3	9	6	1	2
6	7	8	3	5	1	2	4	9
3	9	5	2	4	8	7	6	1
2	1	4	6	9	7	8	3	5
5	3	2	9	7	4	1	8	6
7	8	1	5	6	1	4	9	3
9	4	6	1	8	3	5	2	7

p.112 SLOPING CURSIVE LETTERS

ACROSS
2. Alice
4. *Love Story*
5. Dylan Thomas
6. *The Albatross*
7. *The Great Gatsby*
11. *So High School*
13. *The Scarlett Letter*
14. the lakes
15. Peter Pan

DOWN
1. Humpty Dumpty
3. *champagne problems*
8. Eve
9. *All Too Well*
10. *illicit affairs*
12. *A Tale of Two Cities*

p.114 BAD BLOOD

Catastrophe's weapon is a lipstick and her nemesis is Arsyn.

Frostbyte's weapon is an icicle and her nemesis is Headmistress.

Mother Chucker's weapon is an axe and her nemesis is Knockout.

Slay-Z's weapon is a gun and her nemesis is Cut Throat.

		Weapon used				Band of Bombshells member			
		Lipstick	Gun	Axe	Icicle	Arsyn	Headmistress	Cut Throat	Knockout
Super Squad member	Catastrophe	X				X			
	Frostbyte				X		X		
	Mother Chucker			X					X
	Slay-Z		X					X	
Band of Bombshells member	Arsyn	X							
	Headmistress				X				
	Cut Throat	X							
	Knockout		X						

p.116 SNAKES AND STONES

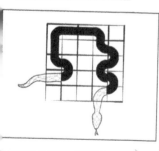

p.117 SPELLING VAULT

8-letters: Midnight

7-letters: Dimming, Minding, Minting

6-letters: Timing, Mining

5-letters: Might, Mimic, Minim

4-letters: Midi, Mind, Mint, Mitt, Mini

p.118 LABYRINTH

p.119 SINGONYMS

1. False God
2. It's Nice To Have A Friend
3. the last great american dynasty
4. invisible string
5. champagne problems
6. no body, no crime
7. Lavender Haze
8. Vigilante Shit
9. Sweet Nothing
10. Fresh Out The Slammer
11. 'tis the damn season
12. the tortured poets department
13. But Daddy I Love Him

p.120 STAY IN STYLE

p.122 THROUGH THE ERAS

G. Release of her first single, *Tim McGraw*: 19 June 2006

D. Release of first album, *Taylor Swift*: 24 October 2006

A. Grammy Awards where Taylor was nominated for her first Grammy, in this instance for Best New Artist: 10 February 2008

I. Taylor wins best Music Video at VMAs and Kanye storms the stage: 13 September 2009

N. Grammy Awards where Taylor won her first Grammy: 31 January 2010

K. Record broken for the fastest selling digital single in history with *We Are Never Ever Getting Back Together*: 14 August 2012.

H. *Shake It Off* becomes Taylor's first song to debut at number 1 in the US charts: 6 September 2014

F. Taylor wipes clean all her social media accounts: 18 August 2017

L. Taylor releases her first re-recorded album: *Fearless (Taylor's Version)*: 9 April 2021

B. First date of The Eras tour: 17 March 2023

M. Taylor named *TIME's* Person of the Year, and the first to be recognized for 'achievement in the arts': 6 December 2023

C. Taylor wins Album Of The Year at the Grammys for *Midnights*, making her the first artist to win that award four times: 4 February 2024

E. *Forbes* declares Taylor a billionaire: 2 April 2024

J. the tortured poets department album released: 19 April 2024

p.124 CRYPTIC CROSSWORD

ACROSS

3. Ice Spice
6. Pennsylvania
7. *Anti-Hero*
8. *Speak Now*
9. Jack Antonoff
10. Grammy

DOWN

1. *reputation*
2. *The Vaults*
4. *Shake It Off*
5. *Billionaire*

p.128 STUMBLING HOLOGRAMS

The date with Chloe took place in Brooklyn, New York at a bar. 13 memories of Taylor surfaced.

The date with Sam took place in Brixton, London at a concert venue. 75 memories of Taylor surfaced.

The date with Sophie took place in Soho, London at a chicken shop. 5 memories of Taylor surfaced.

The date with Marcus took place in Hollywood, Los Angeles at a vinyl record shop. 8 memories of Taylor surfaced.

		Date location				Venue				Memories surfaced			
		Brixton, London	Soho, London	Brooklyn, New York	Hollywood, Los Angeles	A chicken shop	A pub	A concert venue	A vinyl record shop	5	8	13	75
Character	Chloe			X								X	
	Sam	X						X					X
	Sophie		X			X				X			
	Marcus				X				X		X		
Venue	A chicken shop		X							X			
	A pub			X								X	
	A concert venue	X											X
	A vinyl record shop				X						X		
Memories surfaced	5		X										
	8				X								
	13			X									
	75	X											

p.130 ENDGAME

You are a mastermind and karma will take you to the summit.

ACKNOWLEDGEMENTS

The Alice Ryrie: *Dr Legendress Supreme Beyond Wildest Dreams*

Louis Whyte-Smith: *Expert Swiftie Extraordinaire*

Diana Ensor: *Iconic Mother of Author, Expert Iconographer, and Author of Countless Best Days*

Sir Weena Brett: *Editrice in Chief and All Round Whizzkid*

Jonny Woodbridge: *Chief Puzzle Innovator*

Megan McLaren: *Madamoiselle Logique Mastermind*

Cecily Cocks: *Crossword Prodigy Princess*

Zara Goozee: *Advanced Ingenuity Consultant*

Chantal Kijak: *Masterful Slaystress*

Doug Harper: *Director of Original Cryptic Kookiness (DOOCK)*

Emilia Carslaw: *Senior Cryptic Consultant*

Abi Harrison: *Swift Enthusiasm Lead*

Jenny Davies: *Detective Sudoklu Advisor*

Sarah Caroll: *President of Flare and Fanhood*

Jacques Morris: *Senior Games Executive*

Lucy Woodbridge: *Chairwoman of Cheerleading*

Kaya Ensor: *Senior Pep Producer*